# Boot Camp

## Basic Training for Your Dog

### Ted Sutton

### Illustrated by Patti Miller

**Detselig Enterprises Ltd.**
**Calgary, Alberta, Canada**

Boot Camp: Basic Training for Your Dog
© 1994 Ted Sutton

Canadian Cataloguing in Publication Data

Sutton, Edward Ian.
 Boot Camp

ISBN 1-55059-085-5

1. Dogs – Training. 2. Dogs – Psychology. I. Title.
SF431.S87 1994    636.7'0887   C94 – 910568–6

*Detselig Enterprises Ltd. appreciates the financial support for our 1994
publishing program, provided by the Department of Canadian Heritage,
Canada Council and the Alberta Foundation for the Arts, a beneficiary of
the Lottery Fund of the Government of Alberta.*

Detselig Enterprises Ltd.
210, 1220 Kensington Road N.W.
Calgary, Alberta T2N 3P5

Illustrations by Patti Miller

Cover design by Dean MacDonald

Printed and bound in Canada
ISBN              1-55059-085-5              SAN 115-0324

*To my family, for their love and support. To my dogs; Kip, Roy and the gang, for enriching my life more than I deserve and to my wife Kate, for being Kate and that means just about everything. And to Al for challenging me to write this book.*

Other books in Detselig's *Life Line* series:

# *Contents*

# Introduction

**Y**ou may have worn a disguise at the checkout stand when you purchased this book. It may even have come in a brown paper wrapper. Not everyone wants to admit that their dog is not a good citizen. Whether your dog has a long history of delinquency or is just starting his training, this book helps you teach your dog how to be well-behaved and a pleasure to have around.

Imagine, no more laps around the parking lot at the grocery store as your dog acquaints himself with the neighbors; no more apologies to the postman as you coax him down from the nearby tree and no more visits to the chiropractor to have your shoulder reset after taking your dog for a walk . . . or is that a tow? Perhaps now you can invite company to visit without risking assault and battery charges resulting from your dog's enthusiastic welcome! A slight exaggeration? I've known actual cases like this. However, even if you just want a more obedient dog who heels properly or lies down on command, this book will guide you in accomplishing your goal.

Even if you have never trained a dog before, you *can* do it, no matter how green your dog is or old he is or how bad he may have been in the past.

This book is designed to be fun. **In less than 10 hours**, you should be proud of your dog and how he behaves. He should walk at your side, "Heel, Sit, Stay, Lie down, Come" – on command. As your training advances, you will notice a significant change in his overall demeanor. He will become more settled and comfortable in his environment. He will become more attentive to what you say and do. He will become more willing to accept your directives. In short, he will be a happier dog.

By the way, this book works on female dogs (bitches) as well as males. I would not want it thought that this is a gender-specific book. The fact is I do not type well (two fingers being my limit) and typing he/she every time seems a lot of work. I hope your dog isn't too offended.

The contents are divided into four chapters containing a total of ten lessons. Each lesson is designed to teach a specific set of skills. Many of the lessons require repetition before you and your dog should expect mastery and before you move on to the next step. The lessons are intended to be incremental, so follow the steps in order. Each lesson builds on the skills acquired in previous lessons. You should feel comfortable with the idea of review and even go back several lessons if or when you run into difficulties.

To verify your new-found abilities, each chapter includes a review test. The idea is not to give you a nervous breakdown but rather, to give you the confidence to carry on to the next level. If you find difficulty with these reviews, try to identify the areas of weakness and repeat those lessons.

There is a significant difference between training the juvenile dog (6 – 12 months of age) and training the mature dog (over one year old). Therefore, I refer to both these age groups separately. As a result, some lessons differ, particularly with regard to correction. The reason that both age groups are addressed is that while most obedience schools are filled with juvenile dogs, the owners of mature dogs have a right to some revenge as well. Since most lessons are presented from these two points of view, be sure which category your dog falls into. If he is exactly 12 months, read both sections since, like most teenagers, he will exhibit behavior relevant to both categories.

Too many times I have noticed beginning trainers with their books in one hand and a dog in the other, trying to find their place in a lesson. Therefore, the summary of each lesson is on a separate page, entitled "Schedule". You can copy the page and take it with you when training your dog. It is designed to give you a quick breakdown of the lesson so that you don't have to fumble with a book and a dog at the same time. Take as many lesson summary pages as you think you will need for any one session. Write on this book, make notes, even draw pictures, whatever works for you.

A word of caution, actually several. This program is designed to train your dog to obey a specific set of commands with a high degree of reliability. If you eventually want to make a working dog, such as a Border Collie herding cattle or a hunting dog such as a Labrador, you may want to temper this regime with a bit of fun with herding or hunting activities. "Softer" dogs may become so comfortable with basic obedience that it becomes difficult to convince them to take risks with their behavior. I train Border Collies and I have found that to go through obedience training without fixing the *desire* to herd has occasionally left me with a dog that will not take the initiative. In a herding dog, that is a *very* serious flaw; so in herding dogs, I like them a little bit bad when I first take them to stock.

It is not true that you "can't teach an old dog new tricks." If your dog is much older than 12 months, you will find a certain resistance to your new intentions. After all you are the same person that might not have objected to him sleeping on the couch or running after the birds in the park. It is important to appreciate that no book can address all the personalities comprising the dog world, and that changing previously established patterns is more difficult than starting fresh with a new puppy. (However, it is not impossible.) As a result of this puppy/adult dog difference, most chapters include a short section dealing with common problems. Many of these glitches are relevant mainly to the older dog. Please read them over before you start your lesson as forewarned is frequently forearmed.

While this book does not focus on specific behavioral problems such as biting or house training, you will find that most minor behavioral problems diminish and usually disappear completely with the introduction of basic training. There are a number of books dedicated solely to the correction of a series of specific problems. If the specific problem behavior you are seeing in your dog does not improve dramatically within the first four or five lessons, do a little extra research. It may be a problem beyond the scope of this book or it may be related to a physical problem such as poor eyesight or hip dysplasia.

Enjoy your sessions with your dog. Training is both fun and rewarding – especially when you win! Remember, when training your dog, "Don't get mad, get even."

Perhaps now would be a good time to put on a pot of tea or coffee. This next chapter is mostly theory, so get comfortable and put your feet up.

# 1

# Principles
# of
# Basic Training

It is probably best to think of your dog as a friendly opponent. A worthy adversary he is! His ambition in life is not to follow you around while you show off to your friends and neighbors. No, his goal in life is far more hedonistic. He is more inclined to goof off, eat well and do pretty much what he feels like.

The theory is that the dog evolved from the wolf family. While there are many other families of wild dog in the world, what makes the wolf unique is that until recently, his was the only family of dog known to hunt in a hierarchical, organized fashion. The wolf pack has a general, officers and soldiers. It has a pecking order, with some dogs giving orders and some dogs taking orders. Hunting is done according to a plan, with chasers, herders and killers all having a specific role to play.

The significance of all this is that your pet lying on the chesterfield over there is a descendant of those killers and soldiers. Most important of all is the fact that his ancestors received and executed orders with such skill that they rose to the top of their food chain. Much of that propensity still resides in your dog today. You can take advantage of his own instincts to follow orders. All that you have to do is convince him you are the boss dog even though at this point he may think he is.

It has been said of politics that "power hates a vacuum." The same is true of the relationship between you and your dog. In his mind, if you are not the boss, he must be. **Therefore, the most basic of all training principles is that you must be in control.** *You must be the leader.*

To be a leader is not all that difficult but you must be attentive to the fact that your dog will expect you to assume this responsibility essentially all the time you are with him. In the dog world, a leader is usually the smartest and toughest of the group. As long as one dog possesses both of these qualities, the leadership will rest with that individual.

I remember one time, several years ago, when my dog Kip and I were trying to work a small flock of sheep through a gate in a stockdog competition. Things were not going well. I would whistle Kip this way and that, up and back, all to no avail. The sheep were not going through the panels. Finally, after what seemed like hours, Kip stood up out of his crouch, gave me a dirty look and started to head off the course. I called to him and told him to stand. I stopped trying to work him for a moment and took a look around. No wonder the sheep were not co-operating – I was standing in the gate!

Once I stepped out of the way (surprise, surprise) Kip moved the flock through the rest of the course with relative ease. Afterward, an elderly Scotsman stepped over to strike up a conversation. Following a good laugh over my latest humiliation, I asked him what he thought were the most important aspects of training.

He said, "Before ye kin train a Collie laddie, first ye must be smarter than the dug."

It is true that the strongest will assert themselves in a pack situation. What we have all seen on these wildlife television programs looks very ferocious indeed, even brutal. It is also true that a superiority in strength is a great training advantage; but our greatest advantage lies in our intelligence, not in brute strength. Leadership, more than anything else, is dependent on intelligence.

## Causes of Disobedience

Your dog is disobedient for three basic reasons:

1. Ignorance
2. Fear
3. Defiance

It is important that you develop the ability to recognize which one of these causes represents the root of the problem at any given time. The cause of disobedience determines the proper reaction on your part. Let us look at these causes and the roles you should play in response.

## *Ignorance*

I like to teach young puppies to come when they are called at a very early age. I do this by taking small pieces of cheese and offering it to the 6 – 8 week old pup. Within three or four times, the pup has begun to associate his name with the cheese. At this point, most puppies will come to their name. I may do this ten times before I start to withhold the cheese and offer it only one time in two or possibly three. This exercise is part of a larger initiative to start the socialization process in the puppy. It is not a serious attempt to train the animal to come when he is called. However, it does serve to illustrate a point – ignorance can be quickly overcome for most of the simple tasks we wish to accomplish.

After a few days of coming when he is called, the pup usually experiments with refusal. I will call the pup and he will not eat the cheese when offered or he may not come without some additional encouragement. To my mind, the pup is saying that he already has the idea of the command but now wants to know if I am prepared to enforce it.

Ignorance, therefore, requires teaching. The role you should take is one of teacher. Try to set up the situation so that your dog will do the task the right way and then encourage that behavior. There are a number of ways for you to make it easy for your dog to do the right thing and difficult for him to do the wrong thing. Follow correct behavior with a reward, be it a pat on the head or vocal praise or a treat. You do not have to reward correct behavior every time, only often enough to achieve consistent repetition of the task.

In most cases, the lessons are designed to teach first and enforce later. The most common way to teach is through positive and negative reinforcement of simple tasks.

It is helpful to have an idea of how long a certain task should take to teach because there is a point at which you begin to wonder if your dog is stupid or unwilling. By the same token, there is no point in punishing your dog if the problem is not defiance but ignorance. As a general rule, stay in "teacher mode" until you are *sure* that your dog has the picture, rather than assuming defiance is the cause of the problem.

### *Fear*

I believe that fear is a far more common cause of disobedience than most folks think. Fear can range all the way from terror to lack of confidence. Fear is quite difficult for the beginning trainer to judge. In its more extreme form, fear often results in aggression, for which the fear biter usually receives a severe pounding. The result? Your dog may now be trained to respond to fear with aggression.

Body language tells you what your dog is thinking. Be a student of body language and work on its vocabulary. Try not to confuse fear for defiance, or even lack of confidence for cowardice. For example, the dog that draws back and shows you teeth is likely doing so out of fear, while a dog that stands upright, raises his hackles and shows you teeth is telling you to "take a long walk off a short pier!" Either dog may bite you if you push it and both are going to hurt if they do, but your reaction to these situations should be quite different.

I have had several dogs that would show teeth when you scolded them – like a foolish grin. After a while they would grin on command or when they were trying to get on my good side. Oddly, on numerous occasions strangers thought the dog was threatening them. Nothing could have been further from the truth. I was surprised these people could not read the body language that went with the smile and know right away that the dog was not threatening anyone.

Contrary to popular anthropological opinion, humans are not the only ones capable of telling lies. Dogs can too. Some will fake any number of symptoms, including deafness, confusion and in some cases, fear.

Dogs don't "tell" fibs often, particularly the young ones. As a result, I usually accept what they tell me at face value until I have good reason to suspect otherwise. Some dogs never lie, others often do – a little like people.

When trying to figure out the cause of disobedience in a given circumstance, I first try to eliminate ignorance or fear before I assume that defiance is the cause.

If I believe the cause is fear, I encourage the dog in an upbeat manner, saying, "good dog!" or "yes, yes" or "that's it, that's it." I also stop the program more frequently to fuss and pat the dog. Breaking the program with two to three minutes of play helps. Keeping the training program short is extremely important, as is review of previously learned skills.

If the fear persists more than a few seconds or if the dog begins to lose control, he will stop thinking and start reacting on instinct. This is more common in juveniles than mature dogs. If verbal encouragement isn't working, stop the lesson. Allow the dog to compose himself. Go back to a previous lesson, something the dog does well, and give that lesson for two to three minutes. After he gets his confidence back, reintroduce your new material – keep it short!

From time to time, I meet someone who is a victim of what I call "The Love Syndrome." This person is of the opinion that because they love their dog, their dog should love them back; and because their dog loves them, he should automatically be obedient. I have never seen anything in the real dog world to support this theory. What a good relationship with your dog will do is reduce both the incidence and degree of the fear reaction. The bonding process, or whatever you want to call it, increases the dog's confidence in you. He knows what your reactions are like. He knows what "good dog" and "bad dog" mean and he probably has a good idea of who is the boss in your relationship.

When I get a dog in for training, I always allow for some time to bond. Not because it makes them *more obedient* but because it makes them *less fearful*. The result of having a dog that has bonded is: your lessons will be more successful, you will require less backtracking and review and you encounter less fear during the program.

Mutual confidence and respect are key to truly great performances by man and dog. The dogs with whom I have had the greatest success were all dogs that I was fond of. The mutual confidence and respect that formed the basis of that affection came after the obedience training – not before. Bonding is good but don't fall for the Love Syndrome.

I do not want to get into semantics over what does or does not constitute "love." I feel a real affection for my dogs and I believe that affection is returned, sometimes ten-fold. I think most dog owners feel the same way. However, affection and obedience are not the same thing, nor will the first result in the second.

## *Defiance*

Outright defiance is probably the least common cause of disobedience and yet the most commonly assumed cause among non-trainers. Defiance happens when a dog refuses a command for no reason other than a contest of wills or because he thinks he can get away with it.

Defiance requires immediate consequences. However, the consequences don't always have to be severe. The problem I have with beatings, aside from the animal welfare issue, is that all too often they simply do not work. The beating can usually be avoided in favor of more successful tactics such as intimidation, brief physical pain, mental pressure or even good old-fashioned persistence.

Kip, before he died, became quite deaf but there was a transition period where I wasn't quite sure if he could hear me or not.

When Kip was about 12 years old, he began to have difficulty hearing whistle commands at long distances. When this first happened, I restricted his use to short work loading cattle or gathering sheep from nearby. He still loved the work and for a while things went smoothly. By the time he was 13, Kip started to tire quite easily but instead of slowing down or stopping he would pretend not to hear. After a short rest he could hear just fine again. The old faker was smart enough to know that being tired wasn't accepted as an excuse but not hearing would stop things in a hurry! I was never positive when he was faking and when he wasn't so I decided to retire him. To this day, I do not know just how often I was outsmarted.

One day, my wife and I took Kip for a short walk along the beach. We were walking along the sand when a family passed us heading out on the low tide. The next thing I knew, Kip had done a 180° turn and followed the children into the shallow water. I called him a couple of times but he couldn't hear me. I thought, "To hell with it, they'll come back in a few minutes." Well they didn't. My wife and I had a short conference and decided we weren't doing anything anyway so we would stop and smell the roses (actually it was rotting seaweed). She said, "Lord knows he's waited for you often enough."

Eventually, the family returned with the old dog trotting along with the kids. I thanked them for walking my dog and we headed home. I couldn't get mad at him anymore and he knew it. A couple of months later he died in his sleep – one of the best dogs I ever had and a good friend.

The key to overcoming defiance is to stop it before it gets started. In other words, get the issue of who is running the show over with while you have the dog on a leash in the early stages of training. A quick sharp jerk of the chain will tell him, "that behavior is not tolerated." If he wants to make an issue of it, he can fight the chain all he wants – the only thing he is doing is hurting himself.

Hesitation, that short period where the dog is still deciding on the wisdom of defiance, can often be overcome with a low growl or a change in posture. Once the sin has been committed, I react swiftly with a short burst of pain

– usually a jerk on the chain. Think of it as a spanking as opposed to a beating. It should be over quickly and there should be no further hard feelings. Don't nag and don't sulk. Get it over with.

## Off-Leash Work

The transition from leash to off-leash work is a big one. It is not uncommon to find that eventually you have to deal with defiance after a period off the leash, particularly when working at a great distance.

In my case, each student seemingly wanted to test the theory that I was too old and fat to run across the field and make my point. If you do not prove your dog wrong the first time he tries this, you will have lost much control.

My dogs are usually half right on this theory. I don't run so much as quick walk to where they are. No commands, no shouting – just me. The tactic is intimidation, which usually results in the dog running away. But where to? Your dog's dilemma is to find a hiding place (we are dealing with fear now). He will likely execute one of two plans: either go home to hide, or drop down and submit. In the latter case, when I get there, I usually grab him by the nose and give it a shake and a pinch, then I pick him up and shake him again (if he's not too big). Either way, what I am looking for is submission. When a dog rolls over or turns his head away he is saying "I give." How rough you get depends on the dog. (We will talk about different types of dogs later.)

In the event your dog heads for home, you are in for a walk. Sometimes, I have walked for 45 minutes before he cracked under the pressure and headed for home. Remember, what caused him to head home was fear, not defiance. Therefore, your punishment should be the same whether your dog runs or stays.

Immediacy is more important than severity since it is very important the dog associates the punishment with the action. The only way I know of to administer immediate punishment in a situation such as this is either with an electric collar or a set up where the dog hurts himself. In most cases, the very fact that you have started for your dog is sending the right message.

You can make life a little easier on yourself by setting this situation up. Try not to have this problem too far from home or where your dog can get hurt.

Dogs can get cagy, just like Kip. They will eventually learn to cheat. Of course some are worse than others. Cheating should be considered the same as defiance and treated the same way – not tolerated. But first, be sure he is able to hear and is capable of executing the command.

Once you have completed your training, occasional reinforcement is required. If you have laid the groundwork, you should not see much defiance.

## Confinement

I am a big fan of confinement, both as a training tool and as a means of keeping your dog safe and out of trouble. I have been selling dogs for over 20 years. Based on the feedback I get from my customers, almost half the puppies raised without benefit of confinement are dead before they are two years old. Perhaps Border Collies are worse than other breeds but I suspect not.

If you are letting your dog run loose, you are probably breaking the law. You are putting your dog at risk of injury and even death. Add to that the fact that your dog is now a menace to society. There is no logical argument for allowing your dog to run loose.

I don't mean to suggest your dog doesn't need exercise – he does. A supervised walk of about 20 minutes is sufficient.

On a more basic level, your dog, on his own and loose, develops a sense of independence counterproductive to your efforts to train him. Imagine how you would feel if, after a day of cavorting with nature, stealing garbage and chasing the postman, your master shows up with leash in hand and a keen desire to practise parade drill up and down the alleyway. On the other hand, if this is the big event of the day, your attitude would be quite different.

The dog that spends his day in the house or an apartment essentially meets the criteria for confinement, although you may find that confinement to a single room is necessary for some dogs. Many trainers I know keep their dogs on short chains, approximately three feet (1 metre) long, attached to a doghouse. I kennel mine in about 100 square feet (10 sq. metres) of space with a doghouse set inside. As far as I am concerned, either system works well and both provide a level of confinement which supports your training program. It is also important that dogs can see what is going on around them and are not too isolated from the normal comings and goings of the day. Your dog should be comfortable in his surroundings with adequate water and functional shelter provided. The idea here is to confine your dog in a comfortable and safe place – not a prison.

Confinement is an important psychological step in preparing your dog for his training. It makes your dog more receptive to the lessons you have planned. Your dog will not be unhappy; on the contrary, he will be more relaxed and in control of himself as he knows that this is his place and nothing bad can happen to him here.

## Pressure and Release

This is another basic principle of training. You apply the command and the pressure at the same time. When your dog obeys, the pressure is released.

For example, there are many ways to teach the Sit command; the simplest and easiest is to command "Sit" and shorten your leash until the dog feels a *mild* choking. As he seeks to relieve the pressure, he will try to sit down. As soon as he does, release the tension and the pressure goes away. **The key is that the dog has relieved the**

**pressure himself**. The next time he is presented with the same problem, he will try the same solution. Soon he will anticipate the pressure with the command and avoid the situation altogether by sitting.

Pressure relies on discomfort and allowing the animal a method to relieve that discomfort. It can be mild or fairly severe, gradual or immediate. It requires advance planning and a means of turning the pressure on and off.

Pressure is NOT punishment. It is used to solicit correct behavior rather than to stop bad behavior. It is used to teach the ignorant dog as opposed to correcting the defiant dog. Pressure may cause a low fear reaction (but often no fear at all), while punishment is generally associated with high levels of fear. Finally, and probably most important, is that it allows the dog to anticipate the pressure with the command and avoid the pressure altogether by immediately obeying. When this happens, don't forget to praise your dog. This adds to the relief and positively reinforces the experience.

Subtle pressure can be put on your dog by such things as tone of voice, posture and cues. Cues are warnings that a specific command is about to be given. They allow your dog to prepare himself to act immediately and thus avoid the heavier pressure about to come.

Many cues are given unconsciously. I had a dog called Roy who taught me that lesson. In a sheep-herding competition there is an exercise called "shedding." The shed is where you cut one sheep away from the rest and have your dog hold (through eye contact) the single away from the rest of the flock. With the dog on one side of the sheep and you on the other, you try to get the sheep lined out in single file with your ribboned ewe at the end of the line. At the point where the second-to-last ewe is going by, call your dog through the gap and then tell your dog to "get up" on the single. This manoeuvre is a meant to show that you and your dog can separate an animal for treatment if she is sick.

On the day in question, I was competing with two dogs. Roy was a great shedder. In fact, he loved to shed so much that he would do it even when he wasn't supposed to. The other dog, Pepper, was a novice and we had practised shedding only a few times. Pepper ran first. She did a good piece of work but had trouble with one old ewe through much of the course. Eventually, the old ewe broke away from the pack and went off course. So much for Pepper.

Roy was next. The problem was, I hadn't forgotten Pepper. On two occasions, I even used Pepper's whistle commands for Roy. That earned me a dirty look! In spite of that, Roy had a good run and I was starting to count my winnings when we got to the shed. The ewes lined out nicely. Boy this was easy! The second to last ewe came up.

Now with Pepper, I had been raising my hand; sort of pointing to the one I wanted. Then I would drop my hand and call her through, all at the same time. Roy, on the other hand, needed no such encouragement. Without even thinking, my hand went up. Roy jumped in with great dash and verve – too early. The second ewe, avoiding the dog, turned right into me! The ewe, the dog and myself landed in a heap. The only prize I got that day was sheep dung on my pants.

Roy was apologetic on the way home but the fault was mine. Be conscious of your cues, they work really well.

Pressure and release, sometimes called "avoidance training," is fundamental to the methods we will be using to train your dog. It requires excellent timing and an ability to anticipate how your dog will respond in given situations.

## Action/Reaction: Timing is Everything

Punishment, pressure/release and praise all depend on timing to be effective. Things have a way of happening quickly during a lesson and it is not uncommon for you to miss opportunities to apply any or all of the above. Therefore, it is important for you to be alert and to try to anticipate possible outcomes. If you can get "in the groove" and stay mentally ahead of your dog, your lessons will go smoothly. If not, confusion and frustration may be the result.

Do your training when you are in the mood. A minimum of three to four lessons a week is the norm but it is equally important that you are mentally up for the exercise. Whether it is morning or afternoon, pick the time best for you. Don't train if you are already cranky, had a bad day at work, are sleepy or have had any alcohol.

The second part of good timing is to watch your dog. He will tell you what he is feeling and in so doing, indicate what he is likely to do next. For instance, the first time you ask your dog to sit he will probably be confused by the pressure – a mild choking sensation. Give him time to think his way out of the situation. Don't immediately hang him from the neck. Instead, put a light tension on the leash that your dog won't perceive as an emergency or a punishment. Give him 20 to 30 seconds to move around a little, in an effort to find a more comfortable position. Be ready to release. Be confident that he will eventually try to sit down. The instant that his rear end starts to go down, release. If he comes back up, put the pressure back on – only a little more this time.

As this process happens, watch your dog. His eyebrows will likely raise, his tail will often come down, he will move his head from side to side. He may even mouth the chain; give it a little jerk if he does. As he tips his head up to get away from the pressure, his hindquarters will start to come down; take a little pressure off. As he starts to sit, take more pressure off. He may show signs of fear or at least concern. Praise him softly. Tell him it's all right. The instant he sits, take all the pressure off and praise him more. As soon as he hears the praise, in his relief, he will probably try to stand. Put the pressure back on.

The whole time this, or any other exercise, is going on, your dog is telling you what he is feeling. You can therefore be prepared to give relief, praise, punishment or pressure depending on what your dog is likely to do next.

The third part of good timing is to set the situation up so that your dog will correct himself. For example, leave a little slack in your leash when you practise heeling. When you turn right and your dog decides to turn left . . . his neck hurts. The slack allows him to make the decision. The fact that he made the wrong decision and hurt himself has nothing to do with you. The timing, in this case, is perfect because you set it up.

Perfect timing is not always possible, but you should strive for it. The more you get it right, the better your training will progress.

## Training Devices

You do not need a huge supply of gadgets to accomplish basic obedience training. Here is a list of the tools of the trade:

- leather collar
- choke collar
- leash
- 40 feet (12 m) of 1/4 inch (.5 cm) cord (long line)
- leather gloves

The leather or nylon collar should be a sturdy one appropriate to the size of your dog. It should be properly sized, allow for two fingers' room between the collar and your dog's neck when done up and have no more than three inches (8 cm) of tongue left over. It should have a ring or clip on which to attach a leash or chain. It should have a strong buckle that neither breaks nor allows for slippage when fastened.

The choke chain must be properly sized. You should be able to slide it over your dog's head with no difficulty. Once around your dog's neck, it should have less than 4 inches (10 cm) of extra chain. The chain should slide through the ring easily, giving a smooth action when you pull on it. **Because it is designed to slide through itself and thus choke the animal, choke chains should not**

**be used to tie a dog. A choke chain is only used during leash work training and removed once the lesson is complete.** To my knowledge, there are no great deals when buying choke chains. A cheap choke chain is often not strong enough and will break when you need it most. Consult your local pet store for types. Their advice with respect to size and strength is likely correct.

A variation on the choke chain is a device called the pinch collar. It is similar to a choke chain except that it has lever-action finger-like projections on the chain. When the chain is pulled, the fingers dig into the neck. Obviously, this is a more severe piece of kit than the ordinary variety. I don't use them much because I have never trained a dog I couldn't control with an ordinary collar. An exception might be a small person with a big dog, if they can't get their dog's attention. If you decide this is the way to go, be sure to get a good collar. Check to see if the pinch devices release when you release tension. Keep them free of hair and debris so they don't stick. Sometimes called "spike" or "prong" collars, they can be **very** severe. The novice handler is often prone to overcorrect and this device can be inconsistent. **Use it with caution**.

The leash can be made of leather, nylon, chain or rope. It consists of a handle at one end and a clip at the other. I prefer the chain leash about 3 feet ( 1 metre) in length. A strong swivel clip is necessary to prevent binding as the dog turns. The handle should be made of leather or nylon webbing. Plastic handles break too easily. Leashes come in a variety of strengths. You probably do not need logging chain for your toy poodle! However, the chain must be stronger than your dog. I prefer the chain types for two reasons. If for some reason you have to tie your dog some place, he can't chew through the chain as he could with leather or nylon. Also, I like to have slack in the leash when I practise heeling. The chain type, because it is heavier, hangs down and gives a better action as you walk.

You see some folks these days walking their dogs with retractable leashes. These are small plastic reels with a nylon lead rolled up inside. Because it is spring loaded, as the dog pulls on the leash it uncoils and when the dog provides slack, the lead will recoil itself. Usually this will give the dog about 15 feet (5 metres) to wander. While I have only used the retractable leash a couple of times, I disagree with the concept. A proper heel will have your dog maintaining a position within about 6 inches (15 cm) of your heel. This gizmo allows for any position within 15 feet (5 m). I think it is dangerous to have that much flexibility in the positioning of your dog, at least to others trying to walk by you. I found it difficult to administer an effective leash correction with this device and it is counter-productive to off-leash training. I do not believe the retractable leash is of much use as a training device. You are probably just as far ahead to use a long line rather than a retractable leash, and your less likely to trip passers by.

The long line is merely an extension of the leash. It should be made of light, strong material. The most economical long line is nylon cord but it can give you a nasty burn, so wear your gloves. The long line is used primarily as a crutch during the transition from leash to off leash. It is also handy when teaching the "Stay" and "Come" commands.

Two other training devices we will not be using much in this book are the whistle and the electric dog collar. The whistle is pretty much a necessity when working at long distances. The electric dog collar is an extremely effective tool but is not for the novice and is quite expensive. But if you are interested in the theories of electric collar dog training, Tri-tronics of Tucson, Arizona puts out a good book on the subject.

Of the endless variety of whistles available, I prefer the Shepherd's whistle. Basically, it is just a piece of plastic folded over with a hole in it. It is a bit difficult to get the thing to make a noise, but after some practice you can blow any combination of pitches and tones. For most trainers, a normal pea whistle works just fine.

## Hard Dogs/Soft Dogs

Dogs come in an endless array of types and personalities; that is both a delight and a challenge. It is always dangerous to try to categorize dogs because of their tremendous variety. Still, it is helpful to predict what their reactions are likely to be, given a certain situation. Also, when first starting a dog, it is sometimes difficult to know just how much pressure should be applied or what the fear reaction will be like or even if defiance is a part of this dog's character. Many questions regarding your dog's personality will be answered during the course of your training program but right now, we don't know quite what to expect.

There are many books on animal behavior. Much of the research is directly related to dogs. If the subject interests you, you can spend many happy hours exploring this aspect of science. In the interests of expediency, we will confine our discussion to the basics as they apply to training.

The expression "hard dog" doesn't refer to a dog that is hard to train but rather to a dog's willingness to accept direction or dominance. Without going into the *whys* and *wherefores*, this type of dog is willful, unwilling to accept dominance and requires greater pressure before accepting a command.

On the negative side, this type is more likely to show defiance and will test you more often than the "soft" dog. He is less likely to accept you as the boss. He is more likely to try to outsmart you and will sometimes sulk when he loses. Generally, he is mentally tough and many people suggest he was the dominant puppy in his litter but I have not always found this to be the case. He usually has a higher pain threshold than soft dogs and can withstand more pressure.

On the positive side, this type of dog usually has a greater level of self confidence. Of the hard dogs that I have standing the pressure of competition. Dealing with fear tends not to be a big problem with this type of dog.

In some ways, a hard dog is easier to train than a soft dog. In fact, many dogs that would be considered hard would not be noticeable by the way they behave. Once trained, they are as happy and manageable as any other. It is just that they should be handled differently than the soft dog largely because they are mentally tougher.

The soft dog can be very biddable and quickly submit to your will. Dealing with fear in this type tends to be a bigger problem than dealing with defiance. They are easy to dominate, even overdominate. Their self-confidence is often lower. They require more positive reinforcement, less punishment and more subtle pressure.

Once trained, the soft dog is great for long-distance work. He will be less likely to cheat or defy your commands. Self-confidence tends to be the biggest problem. It is important for you to recognize when this dog is losing confidence and be quick to praise him. Keeping your lessons short is extra important with this type.

When referring to hard vs. soft dogs, I am not referring to their intelligence, ability, talent, physical strength or size or even their heart. I am referring to their responsiveness to pressure. Obviously, the range from hard to soft is on a continuum. While there are extremes at either end, most dogs appear to fall somewhere in the middle.

I like working with both personalities and have been fortunate to have good dogs of both types. If you can accurately identify the extent to which your dog falls into one of these categories, your job is much easier, because you will be better able to predict the reactions you will be dealing with.

## The Advantage of Strength: Who has It?

So far, I have argued that intelligence is your greatest advantage, but the advantage of strength is also quite useful.

Unfortunately, not everyone is stronger than their dog. If this is the situation, you may have to adopt a slightly different strategy. Some possible ways to make up for lack of strength are either to seek a mechanical advantage such as the pinch collars or develop a knowledge of your dog's soft spots. For example, if you have a dog that wants to jump up on you, bring your knee up so that he takes it in his chest. If the dog is either too big or too small for that tactic, grab his toes when he gets up on you. Squeeze them together and make a growling noise. Soon, even a big dog will stop putting his toes where they don't belong.

A bitch disciplines her puppies during the early stages of their lives. The lessons learned at the hand of the mother are not soon forgotten. One of the things a bitch does when scolding her babies is to grab their muzzle in her mouth, squeeze a little (or a lot) and growl. Even the biggest dogs get the message when you mimic this. While they may choose not to take heed, it won't be because they didn't understand the message.

The opposite problem arises when you have a huge strength advantage over your dog. Now you have the potential to do serious damage. To cause serious pain is not the normally desired effect in most situations arising from our lessons. You may wish to do away with the choke collar in favor of the leather one. You may choose to keep the choke collar and be careful with it. Whatever you decide, remember that when you have a great strength advantage, you need to know just how hard you have to be to make your point.

## Managing the Situation

The idea of lesson planning may seem like a great deal of work just to outsmart old Marmaduke but it can pay big dividends.

It snows a lot where I live. Many years ago, my neighbor was a trainer of Chesapeake Bay retrievers. Sometimes, I would help Jim with his training. The basic idea with retrievers is to go **straight** from the handler to the bird. In the winter, he would lay a snowmobile track about a half mile long and straight as an arrow. I would stand at various points along the snowmobile trail and when Jim fired the shotgun, I would throw the dummy into the air so that it landed close to the trail. The snow on the trail would be packed fairly hard so that the dog would stay on top. If the dog went off the trail he was breaking powder snow.

Without any fuss or trouble, Jim taught his young retrievers the value of going straight by making it easy to do it right and difficult to do it wrong. Jim was an expert at managing a situation to his advantage. By being a little crafty, using the lay of the land and maybe the help of a friend, you too can become an expert.

When planning a training session, keep an eye out for possible situations that you can use to your advantage. Take one of the simplest as an example: suppose you are teaching the heel command. The idea will be to have your dog follow on your left heel. If your dog has a tendency to cross over behind you, (and many do) walk alongside a fence or along a curb in a manner that makes it difficult if not impossible for the dog to be comfortable on the right-hand side.

This kind of pressure is so subtle, your dog won't even notice you are doing it to him. In many cases, this is the best kind of pressure of all.

When things aren't going well and you seem to be losing the fight, don't get mad. Get crafty and get even. Often, when you meet with successful opposition it is because you aren't doing enough planning. Think about what you problem is over a cup of coffee and plan a strategy that gives you the advantage. Back up a lesson or two and repeat them in order to reestablish your control. Review what you have learned to date and what your dog is telling you just before things started to go wrong. From that point, try to devise a plan that makes it hard on the dog when he does it incorrectly and easy when he does what you want.

Enlist the help of confederates if necessary. Make it a game – one that you will win.

A fellow Border Collie trainer used to have a great dog named Scot. Scot was a powerhouse of a dog, a bit on the hard side. My friend loaded up his dog one day and drove four hours to my place with a plan! Scot had been working for a number of years and was of the opinion that when he was more than a quarter mile away he didn't have to stop on the whistle command. The next morning, I cut about six feet of a poplar branch and went out into a field of grass where the grass stood about a foot tall. My branch and I laid down in the designated place, about 40 feet behind a small flock of grazing sheep. My friend sent Scot out for the sheep. As Scot came around behind the sheep and with his back to me, I heard the whistle to stop. I jumped up with a roar and slapped the branch down on ole cheating Scot . . . GOTCHA! About ten years later, Scot had to be put down and in all the time since that day, he never once cheated on his stop behind the sheep.

The point is, most of the best corrections result from planning. A real good correction is often the last correction.

## Reinforcement

For the sake of discussion, let's agree to consider reinforcement as falling into one of three basic types: positive, negative and long overdue.

It is absolutely normal for a dog to backslide after a while. The "Sorry, Boss, I forgot" happens after a period of layoff. Mostly this occurs because you start to slack off and your dog learns to cheat; a little at first and then a lot.

The cure doesn't have to be a beating. Instead, briefly repeat the lessons already learned and expect a high standard of performance following the completion of your training. At first, revisit your training program about once every two weeks. Go through the whole program and demand perfection. Later, about once a month should be sufficient to keep your dog where you want him.

Webster defines reinforcement as "to strengthen by additional assistance." In our case we want to increase the probability of a correct response or decrease the probability of an incorrect response through additional stimuli. The idea being if the response results in a pleasant experience, the response is *more* likely to be repeated; if the response is followed by an unpleasant experience, the response is *less* likely to be repeated.

So far, we have talked mostly about negative reinforcement. I wouldn't want you to start your lessons thinking that was the only tactic available to you. Positive reinforcement works, especially on soft dogs. Constant cooing and crooning may make you feel like an idiot but the soft dogs love it. You will build up their confidence and make the whole exercise fun for them. Personally, I prefer a quiet place where no one but my dog can hear but some folks don't suffer from these inhibitions. Whatever your pleasure, try it – your dog will love you for it.

## Tactics for Getting Your Way

A few last thoughts before we get underway. Apart from all the suggestions made so far, there are a couple of extras you should know about.

Using a low voice and dropping it into a growl is pretty much what mom did before hanging a beating on junior. Junior still remembers these lessons. If you want to make a quick correction, try a growling "Noooo!" or "Get outta that". You will be surprised how well it works. Get your voice as low as possible. Imitate a growl.

Pushing your dog to the ground and growling or grabbing his nose is another lesson Fluffy already understands. Soft dogs are quite sensitive to these kinds of correction – perhaps they got beaten up more by their littermates.

Using phrases such as "that'll do" for quit and "stop that noise" for barking seems to work better than the one word commands. I think it is because the dog can more accurately identify a phrase than a single word. Feel free to add a couple of words to a command.

A person crouching is a threatening posture to a puppy. **When calling a puppy, try lying down instead**.

Leaning forward over a dog is also somewhat intimidating, as is stepping toward him. Use these postures as a mild threat when you need it. Of course, if you are constantly doing it without ever following through on the threat, your dog will become desensitized.

Most dogs don't care for eye contact. Making eye contact further strengthens your message and if possible, should be used when making a strong correction.

## Summary

You are probably anxious by now, to get started with your training. Hopefully, you will have gathered the basic ideas behind the training you are about to do. Please feel free to review this chapter from time to time as you may want to refresh your memory prior to planning future lessons.

# 2

# Teaching
## Your Dog to Heel

**T**he objective of the heel command is to have your dog walk beside you with his head approximately at the side of your knee. The dog should maintain this position on a slack leash (eventually off leash altogether) at any speed or direction you choose.

Normally, you would train your dog to walk on your left side. If you are left-handed, you may prefer the right side. Also, if you plan to be walking two dogs at once, you may want to train one for the left and the other for the right.

The lessons for this skill are designed from two different points of view. Schedule A (p. 44) is for the juvenile dog (6 – 12 months of age). Schedule B (p. 45) is for the older dog (over 12 months of age). Read the following section, paying particular attention to the schedule that applies to your dog.

# Lesson 1
# Basic Leash Work

Juvenile dogs tend to be softer than the mature dogs. Therefore, they usually require softer treatment. Mature dogs tend not only to be a bit harder, but they have established some bad habits as well. Therefore, if you have a mature dog, you not only have to teach this new skill, but overcome some of the previously established habits. The good news is that the mature dog can stand more pressure and concentrate on tasks longer than most puppies. Therefore, while this task may take a little longer than with puppies, your overall training in subsequent lessons will be faster.

You need a leash 3 – 6 feet (1 – 2 metres) in length. It must have a swivel clip at one end and a handle for your hand at the other. You also need a leather collar and a choke chain. Both should be fitted to be sure they are the correct size. The choke chain should slip over your dog's head easily, with no more than 3 – 4 inches (8 – 10 cm) of extra chain.

The choke chain allows you to cause fairly significant pain. You may find that starting out with this device, especially if you have never used one before, may be too extreme. I usually start with the leash attached to the leather collar for pups. If I find that I need more severity, I use the choke chain in later lessons. Mature dogs usually start with the choke collar, unless they are very small.

The last piece of equipment required is a pair of leather gloves. Give your equipment a brief check to make sure everything is in working order. Pay particular attention to the choke chain and leash. If they break in the middle of your lesson you have been wasting your time.

## I. Lesson Plan

Every successful lesson has a plan – some are quite devious. Since this is your first effort, let's keep it simple.

Your objectives are:

- to familiarize yourself and your dog with the equipment and the area
- to train your dog to "give" to the pressure of the leash

a) *Location.* A good location for these lessons is quiet and isolated, with few if any distractions. The ground should be level and easy for you to walk on. A fence that you can walk beside is a good feature. Keep away from the traffic. Take the time to locate a good place to do your training. Perhaps drive to the local park to spot a good location.

b) *Length.* It is **very** important to keep the length of your sessions short – no more than ten minutes at first. This session should take about five minutes of actual training time for juvenile dogs and possibly the full ten minutes for mature dogs.

c) *Plan.* The plan is to take your dog to the training site. Once there, put on the choke chain and/or attach your leash to the dog. At first your dog may do nothing, but eventually he will try to walk away. When he does, give the leash a jerk and tell him to "heel." Pull your dog and move your body so that he is in the approximate position to start the heel.

The idea is to have your dog try to get away from the leash pressure and the only way he can do that is to be in the correct position, as shown in Figure 1 (next page).

Once your dog has found the correct position and therefore received relief and praise for doing so, you end the lesson.

d) *Correction.* The idea behind correction is pressure/release. If we talk about punishment, I refer to it as "punishment." In this lesson, we want to rely almost solely on correction. If there is to be any punishment, the dog will do it to himself. The application of correction with a leash should be a swift jerk on the leash followed immediately by release. If your dog does not respond correctly, repeat the procedure. The reason for the jerking motion is that a steady pull on the choke collar will strangle your dog. This is almost guaranteed to cause panic in the puppy. Once they panic, they are learning little – especially when they can't breathe.

*Figure 1*

I have found that the most common reaction to this lesson is *fear*, which in turn usually results in a struggle to get away. While the fear in your pup may be significant, it is unlikely to be full-blown panic. Even so, as long as the pup can breathe, he will come out of it.

e) *Voice*. You should be prepared to modulate your voice in response to the behavior you see in your pup. Praise him in your normal voice but inject enthusiasm into what you are saying. Pat your pup or ruffle his ears, otherwise don't wave your hands around too much.

When he is heading in the wrong direction, lower your voice and give him a low growling "Nooo." Try to get this warning in ahead of your actual correction, but don't wait too long to apply the leash correction. It is okay if you say "Nooo" and jerk, followed immediately by praise.

## II. Execute the Plan

Step 1. If you plan to use a choke collar, put it on by feeding the chain through one of the rings on the end to make a loop. Slip the loop over your dog's head. Take one of the rings and tug on it gently. If the collar tightens like a slip knot, you have the correct ring, if not try the other ring. Make sure that when you release tension the collar slips back to its original diameter. The sliding of the chain should be smooth with no resistance to the tension you apply to it.

Step 2. Clip on the leash. Position your dog in a manner approximating Figure 1. Don't worry if you haven't got it quite right or if you have to move your own body to set it up. Start with about 6 inches (15 cm) of slack in your leash; this creates a comfort zone within which your dog will be praised and not pressured.

When the dog starts to wander off, he will take the slack out of the leash. **Jerk** the leash so that the collar pulls the dog's head back into position. at the same time say "good dog" or something similar.

The reason for the jerk and not a slow pull is that you want to cause some discomfort and you want to put the dog back into position so that he gets relief almost immediately. The pressure and the release should happen so fast that your dog is out of trouble before he even knew he was in it. The reason for saying "good dog" so fast is that by the time you say it, your dog will be back in the comfort zone.

Step 3. From this point on, one of several things are likely to occur. With a soft dog, you might get a whimper and the pup may roll over and submit. If this is the case, add more positive reinforcement by praising and cooing to the dog.

Your pup might panic (fear reaction) and try to flee altogether. In which case, you will be standing with your dog pulling at the end of the leash as far away as he can get. This is a common reaction of juvenile dogs, less common with older dogs. Don't give ground. Instead, with gentle but firm tugs, keep the pressure on your pup. Remember, this is pressure not punishment. The second he steps up toward you (even a couple of inches), give him some release. Allow him 10 to 20 seconds to think about what just happened and then start tugging again. Each time he gives to the leash, allow him a few seconds of release. Continue the process until he has returned to the proper position. You should not end the lesson before he has returned to your side and at no time should you step toward him.

Your dog may simply return to the correct position and wonder what the heck happened. You should be so lucky! If so, continue to praise your dog for a bit. Then just stand quietly until he tries to walk away again and repeat the procedure. The mature dogs often do this at first. They usually think about it for a while and decide what to do about it. If they decide to go along with you on this one – don't worry, they will almost certainly decide to fight in Lesson 2. Now or later, it doesn't matter.

Your dog might, after the first jerk, decide to leave the country by first running one way, then the other. A hard dog may make a concerted effort to break free. If so, hold your ground and jerk him back forcefully. How hard he hits the end of the leash is his problem and he may hit it hard indeed. Every time he turns back to you, praise him. Once he stops trying to race away, start with the gentle tugs as in the previous example.

The juvenile dog may hold out for a little while but generally within a few minutes, gives to the pressure. Mature dogs, on the other hand, have probably been taken for walks before. In that process, they may have learned to lean on the leash and tow you around the park. If that is the case, you probably are in for a fairly long struggle. The major difference in this scenario is that you will likely have to escalate the tugs on the leash until they cause pain. But the process is the same. Jerk hard on the leash (use the choke collar), about one strong jerk every three seconds until he gives to the pressure. Remember, one step toward you should earn him some relief. Also, once he comes to a stop and gets his wits about him, use less severe tugs (as opposed to jerks) on the leash.

Once in a while, you run into a real tough dog, or as a handler you may not be strong enough to cause sufficient discomfort to get the job done. In this case, quit after 10 minutes – no sense being crazy about it. Round One goes to the dog.

If this happens to you, remember the pinch collar. Another idea is to find the biggest person you know and enlist their help. Have them read this section and go back to the training site for Round Two. Stand close beside your helper and give all the voice commands. Let them do the heavy work with the leash. In this specific case only, you should repeat this lesson using your enforcer. Allow 48 hours between lessons and repeat it only once. After that you are going to have to think of some means of achieving mechanical advantage on your own.

One last thing. If/when your dog gets over being frightened and has found the comfort zone, he may still try to get away by going around your legs with the result that you are now tied up with the leash. One more step and you'll fall on your face! Don't call 9-1-1. The problem is that you are being too slow to correct the dog as he moves out of the comfort zone, or you have too much slack in your leash. The temptation is for you to turn around so that you are in the correct position.

That's okay if the idea is for your dog to train you to pirouette. Try shortening up on the leash and anticipating when your dog is about to move. You have to be quick enough to prevent him from getting in front of you or going around behind. You can afford to be fairly gentle with this correction as the dog is just testing the limits of the comfort zone while trying to please you – but it sure looks funny.

Step 4. Once your dog is standing in the correct position, you have made your point. While you don't want to quit until you have had at least one correction, you don't want to belabor the point either. Therefore, if your dog returns to your side and stays there for about one minute, end the lesson. It is not necessary to repeat this lesson. Instead, you should proceed to the next lesson within 24 hours.

# Lesson 1
# Basic Leash Work

---

## Schedule A: Juvenile Dogs

Copy this sheet and take it with you. Check off the items as they are completed:

_____ lesson plan completed

_____ location selected

_____ equipment checked

_____ used your voice effectively

_____ gave corrections effectively (how many?)

_____ gave praise effectively

_____ dog responded correctly (how many times?)

_____ lesson ended on time (five minutes)


ROUND ONE GOES TO . . . (check winner)

_____ ME! (yesss)

_____ DOG (oops)


Question:    Based on his reaction in this lesson, would you say your dog is hard or soft?

Clue:    If you had to use pressure to the point of causing real pain, the answer is probably "hard."

Question:    Do you need to replace any broken or ineffective equipment?

Question:    Was the location suitable for training? Were there distractions?

# Lesson 1
# Basic Leash Work

## Schedule B: Mature Dogs

Copy this sheet and take it with you. Check off the items as they are completed:

_____ lesson plan completed

_____ location selected

_____ equipment checked

_____ used your voice effectively

_____ gave corrections effectively (how many)

_____ gave praise effectively

_____ dog responded correctly (how many times?)

_____ lesson ended on time (ten minutes)

ROUND ONE GOES TO . . . (check winner)

_____ ME! (yesss)

_____ DOG (oops)

Question:   Based on your dogs reaction to this lesson, would you say he was hard or soft?

Clue:   If you did not have to use significant pain to pressure your dog, the answer is probably "soft."

Question:   Do you need to replace any broken or ineffective equipment?

Question:   Was the location suitable for training? Were there distractions?

# Lesson 2
## Introductory Heel
## "Start at the Walk"

Begin by reviewing what you have learned so far about your dog. Review how he reacted to pressure, correction and praise. Determine, in your own mind, the strategy that seemed to work best. Is your dog soft or hard? Did he really pick up when you started to praise him?

When I first became serious about obedience training, I was a teenager. It was NOT COOL to be cooing to a dog! I could do the "jerk the chain" thing well but I had great difficulty with the "praise" thing. To make matters worse, I had a young pup only five months old. She was far too young and soft to be working without praise. Soon, I was frustrated and she was scared half to death.

Eventually, I swallowed my pride, went to a secluded area where none of my friends could possibly hear me, and gave her what she needed, praise. After that we got along famously. She learned quickly and painlessly. I learned that praise is at least as important as correction.

Once you have taken stock of past experience and have come to a sense of balance with respect to correction and praise, you can begin laying the ground work for Lesson 2. Hopefully, your dog has learned a little about giving to the leash. Since we decided not to belabor the point or to repeat the first lesson, chances are your dog will still offer resistance to the leash. At least he should not be as frightened about the whole thing.

This lesson is designed to be repeated. This is the first time we have talked about the need for repetition. Obviously, if your dog is still struggling with a command or, more accurately, a skill, it does little good to proceed to the next lesson. How often a lesson is repeated is something only you can determine. As lessons become more difficult, the need for repetition increases. I indicate how often I think a lesson should be repeated based on my own experience. Please do not take that as either a minimum or a maximum. Some dogs struggle with a simple task only to sail through some of the more difficult ones.

As before, we will go though basically the same process of lesson plan and lesson followed by review.

## I. Lesson Plan

The objective of this lesson is to have your dog maintain the correct heel position (usually on your left side) while walking in a straight line and at one speed (comfortable walking pace).

a) *Location.* Likely, you were able to find a location that suited your purposes during the previous lesson. For this lesson, at least, you should look for an aid to keeping the dog in position. I like to find a stretch of solid fence or hedge row that I can walk beside. By putting my right shoulder close to the fence wall, I can make it virtually impossible for my dog to get over to the right-hand side of me. That being prevented, all I really have to worry about is not letting him get too far in front or behind me during my walk. See what you can do to find such a place. While it is not necessary, it will make things a bit easier. Consider also, the criteria you looked for the last time; good ground, few distractions and no traffic.

b) *Length.* Again, keep your sessions short. Five minutes is ideal. Ten minutes for a mature dog is about the maximum. If your schedule does not allow you to keep these sessions short because you can only train a couple times a week, you might try having about a three-minute session followed by about fifteen minutes of play followed by another three-minute session. This way you may be able to get as many as three sessions in during an evening. Be careful with this. Mature dogs are more likely to be able to do this than the juvenile ones. Nor does this system allow for the dog to truly think about previous lessons. The idea of allowing your dog time think over a lesson is often called "sink in time."

Repetition is also important. Under a normal training regime, I like to train a minimum of three days a week and preferably five days a week. This means you want to set aside 20 minutes a day for training. Repeat lessons until you and your dog have fully mastered them. You should be prepared to repeat this lesson three times. By then you and your dog should be getting a bit bored with the whole thing – which is good! Later, whenever you get into trouble with a task, you and your dog can do a couple of minutes of this lesson to get your confidence back. Believe me, it is going to happen.

c) *Plan.* Take your dog to the training site. Once there, put on the leash and collar (and choke chain if you are using one). If possible start at the fence. At first, do nothing for about 30 seconds. Allow your dog to either get into the groove or try to get away on his own. Hopefully he will stay with you. If not, settle him down with a word or two.

The idea is to walk along the fence at a steady pace, with your dog maintaining the correct position at your left heel. As your dog gets out of position, correct him with a gentle jerk on the leash followed immediately by praise. If your dog persists in towing you along, the jerk should be fairly severe. If he lags behind and you are towing him, you should rely also on praise and excitement to call him into the correct position. Walk up and down the fence line until your dog is able to maintain the correct position for at least 30 feet (9 metres).

When you stop, ask your dog to "Sit." He should do so in the correct position, at your side. However, for this first lesson, let's leave the sit out. We can cover it later. At this point, just let your dog stand by your side. When you start again, ask your dog to "Heel." Lead off with the left foot when you go.

Once your dog is able to maintain the comfort zone by staying in the correct position, you should end the lesson – even if it is very short!

d) *Correction*. The idea here is to set up your comfort zone by having about six inches (15 cm) of slack in your leash. Once your dog has taken that much away, he should experience discomfort. Depending on the severity and the persistence of the dog, the discomfort could range from a low growl to a severe jerk on the chain. Generally speaking, towing or forging ahead is considered a more aggressive behavior than lagging behind. A dog that persists, after a few gentle tugs, in towing you should be clearly corrected. A dog that lags behind is often confused and frightened. At first, your should try praise and call him back into position by saying "good dog" or making a clicking sound like you would do to a horse. If that doesn't work use tugs on the leash to keep the pressure on. Only provide comfort when he is in the correct position.

e)*Voice*. This lesson is usually most successful when using an upbeat approach and lots of praise. The soft dogs need the praise and even the hard dogs need to figure out where the comfort zone is. The best way to let them know when they are in the right place is through the slack in the leash combined with a positive voice.

The low growling "Nooo" can be used effectively for dogs that start to forge ahead and tow. You have to be quick about this though, as it should be done **before** the dog is out of the zone. You need to be able to anticipate.

## II. Execute the Plan

*Note: The following instructions assume you are teaching your dog to heel on your left side. If you want him to heel on the right, reverse positioning directions.*

Step 1. Unless they are extremely soft or small, mature dogs should get the choke chain. Extra hard juveniles should also have the choke chain put on. The reason for this is that you should have some feel for how much is required to cause pain by now and be able to avoid it if you want, while at the same time, dogs that tow are likely to need a fairly severe correction. Check your equipment to insure that the choke slides properly and the leash will not break.

Step 2. Orient yourself to your fence. Position your dog correctly, even if you have to physically push him into place. While the object of the first lesson was to have your dog giving to the leash and taking the correct position, because we did not repeat that lesson, it is entirely possible that your dog will still struggle with it. Allow about 30 seconds for your dog to get settled. If he starts to wander off, give him a "Nooo" or a jerk if required.

A friend brought me a dog once that was so unruly I couldn't even get to this stage without a huge fight. Even after doing Lesson 1 about three times, if this dog thought he could make a break for it, he did! He was about three years old and really tough. I didn't want to drag him to the fence and I didn't want to start this lesson without the previous one. In the end, I drove him in my car up to the fence as close as I could get. I put on the leash and choke collar, got out of the car and went to the passenger door, opened it up and let the rodeo commence!

The point of this little story is just do the best you can. Once you get into position, the advantage is yours.

Step 3. In most of your training you will provide your dog with cues, hints to get ready for what is about to come. In this case, the cue for "Heel" is the foot you lead off with. If your dog is to heel on the left, you will lead off with the left foot. You can even cheat a little by putting your left foot forward a little while you are standing.

Once Marmaduke is settled and you have adjusted the slack in your leash to about six inches (15 cm), lead off with your left foot and command in a firm voice "Heel."

Don't stop talking! Encourage your dog to keep up and warn him when he gets too far ahead. Tug on the leash whenever you need to. Many times when a dog starts to lean a bit on the leash, I put half a dozen quick little tugs combined with a growled "Nooo." Most dogs heed this warning and drop back a bit.

Proceed at a leisurely pace. Make it easy for your dog to keep up. This is especially true of juveniles. If you have your fence set up, keep your shoulder as close as is comfortable. If your dog tries to get over to the right side, walk closer to the wall. By trying to get over to your right it is necessary for the dog to also drop behind. Therefore, he should be tugged and coaxed back up to the correct spot.

If you do not have a fence handy, you will have to be especially diligent to prevent the dog from ducking behind you, then across in front. The result of this is that you get tripped by the leash. Preventing this manoeuvre requires that you keep the dog from falling back behind your leg.

Step 4. From the moment you start on your walk, several scenarios are likely to happen. Don't get excited. Most are fairly common reactions.

If you have a soft dog – and this is often the case with juveniles – he may lock up all four wheels and dig in for all he is worth. In my opinion, this is usually a fear reaction. I have had the most luck when I get quite vocal with my encouragement. Often I pat the side of my leg and repeat "good dog, get up, get up." Even "come on Marmaduke, there's a good boy" or "atsa girl, atsa girl." The "atsssa" sound with the elongated "ss" seems to excite dogs and any or all of these usually brings them up to the correct position. When he does come up, in the early stages, occasionally stop to give him a pat. This exercise is just an extension of the first lesson about giving to the pressure of the leash. In this case he hasn't quite under-stood the message yet. Sometimes, the dog is confused because when he gave to the leash before, he got relief and this time because you are moving, relief is harder to get. If you think this is the cause of the problem, slow down and take your time for the first lesson. You can always speed up later.

Your dog may bolt from side to side or back and forward. This may be a sign of a particularly hard dog that is making a determined attempt to break away but more often it is a pronounced fear reaction. If my guess is right, encouraging your pup and slowing things down as in the previous example should work. If what we have is a renegade, the strategy will persist long after you have tried to settle the dog down. In that case, a severe jerk on the leash will cause him to think again. Remember, the jerk should result in the dog bouncing into the correct position, which means he should be praised for being there. Stop and let your dog collect himself and decide if he still wants to play the fool. There are few true renegades among juvenile dogs. Behavior such as this from juveniles is almost always due to fear.

On the other hand, if the mature dog has been towing you around for a while and suddenly you get on this discipline kick, the reaction may well be denial. He may be saying, "You've got to be kidding! I'll go wherever I want!" With the mature dog, behavior such as this often warrants severe correction. Even so, remember to slow things down when you get into these disputes.

Another problem is having your pup jump out ahead and wrap the leash around your legs or lie down in front of you. Shorten your leash to narrow the comfort zone. Hold the leash in your right hand but let the line go through your left. Keep your left hand down on your thigh on the side of your leg. This results in your dog having almost no slack unless his head is right beside your knee. Slow down. Stop every three or four feet ( 1 to 2 metres) to assure him that this is the correct position and that he is okay. Praise him constantly, the whole time he is locked into this position. If he is trying to cross over in front of you, goose-step a little to exaggerate your leg movements and to make it dangerous to cross over. After you have walked 30 or 40 feet (9 or 12 m) this way, stop for a rest and a bit of praise. When you start off again, gradually let more slack through your hand until you are back to your normal six inches. Be quick to warn your dog "Nooo" if he starts to get ahead.

Keep up the praise if he is in the right spot. As you have probably surmised, I usually take this reaction to be mostly fear and confusion and therefore act accordingly. The shortening of the leash is more to provide a crutch so the dog can find his range, rather than being a corrective measure. But the goal of this task is to have your dog eventually heel off leash. This means the crutch is only a temporary measure and must soon be taken away.

<u>Step 5</u>. Repeat your lessons until your dog is always in the correct position, shows no signs of wanting to get away and no signs of fear or confusion. Usually this takes me three or sometimes four, five minute sessions. The heel should be willingly done on a slack leash before moving on to the next lesson. The dog should begin to anticipate the Heel command from your advanced foot cue. As a final phase of this lesson, practise the heel without the aid of the fence.

<u>Step 6</u>. At first you walk a little, stop a little, if for no other reason than to keep things slowed down. By the second or third repetition, your dog should immediately sit by your side when you stop. There are several ways to teach the sit. The method I have found most successful is:

- when you stop, stop on your left foot

- shorten your leash until you are lifting your dog up a bit. Do NOT immediately start to choke him – simply make him a little uncomfortable (see Fig. 2a)

- command "Sit" every 10 seconds and keep the pressure on

- at first your dog will squirm around trying to find a more comfortable position. Eventually (two – three minutes maximum) he will try sitting (Fig. 2b, next page)

- the instant he sits, give him relief (slack off the leash) and congratulate him (Fig. 2c, next page)

*Figure 2a*

*Figure 2b*

*Figure 2c*

- if after two to three minutes he does not try to sit, increase the pressure by lifting up on the leash a bit more. This lifting should NOT be a jerky motion but a slow steady pull

- if after congratulating him, he gets up again, growl "Nooo," say "Sit" and reapply the pressure

- do not make him sit long at first (20 – 30 seconds), then start your walk again

- every time you stop, ask him to sit

- after you have asked him to sit a few times, give the command ONLY ONCE, then apply pressure until he sits

## Summary

As in your first lesson, take note of your dog's behavior. If he is hard and prepared to fight the leash, you will find yourself in for a struggle. If he is soft and falls to the ground or fights the leash out of fear, you will have to do a lot of encouraging to get him to come along. Remember that the juvenile dog is more likely to be softer than the mature dog. Also be prepared to reconsider your earlier assumptions. If you find that leash correction is being escalated into all-out war, try a different strategy. If your earlier assessment is changing from hard to soft, lighten up on your correction and try to be more positive about things.

The same thing holds true the other way. If you started off thinking your dog was soft and would never do anything to challenge you, yet your current strategy of encouragement is not working, increase the pressure by trying the leash correction. Even soft mature dogs can and often do put up a fight if they are used to doing the leading.

# Lesson 2

## Introductory Heel – "Start at the Walk"

### Schedule A: Juvenile Dogs

Copy this sheet and take it with you. Check off the items as they are completed:

_____ lesson plan completed

_____ location selected

_____ equipment checked

_____ used your voice effectively

_____ gave praise effectively

_____ dog maintained the correct position (how long?)

_____ dog sits on command

_____ lesson ended on a positive note and on time (five minutes)

Question: Did you learn anything new about your dog's temperament?

Clue: A great deal can be learned about your dog, including hard vs. soft and even intelligence, during this lesson. Watch for his reaction to pressure and correction.

Question: Do you need to make any changes to equipment or location for your next lesson?

Question: How many times did you have to repeat this lesson?

# Lesson 2
# Introductory Heel – "Start at the Walk"

## Schedule B: Mature Dogs

Copy this sheet and take it with you. Check off the items as they are completed:

\_\_\_\_\_ lesson plan completed

\_\_\_\_\_ location selected

\_\_\_\_\_ equipment checked

\_\_\_\_\_ used your voice effectively

\_\_\_\_\_ gave praise effectively

\_\_\_\_\_ dog maintained the correct position (how long?)

\_\_\_\_\_ dog sits on command

\_\_\_\_\_ lesson ended on a positive note and on time (five minutes)

Question: Did you learn anything new about your dog's temperament?

Clue: A great deal can be learned about your dog, including hard vs. soft and even intelligence, during this lesson. Watch for his reaction to pressure and correction.

Question: Do you need to make any changes to equipment or location for your next lesson?

Question: How many times did you have to repeat this lesson? While a mature dog is usually quicker to get the idea, he is also more likely to resist the whole exercise. Therefore, you may well find that you may have to repeat this lesson more often – six times is not unusual.

# Lesson 3
# Varying Speeds and Direction

Many people are surprised to find just how difficult this is, especially for a young dog. Imagine yourself knee-high to a giant. The fool cannot decide how fast to go or even what direction to take. It would be intimidating to suddenly be expected to anticipate the giant's every move.

This is much more a skill than a contest of wills. So be patient! Keep your lessons short! The exercise is a difficult one – more so for juveniles than mature dogs. If you don't believe me, try following someone who changes their direction and speed without warning.

In time, this skill becomes a bit like the children's games "Simon Says" and "Red Light, Green Light." Your dog will enjoy the challenge.

At first, however, your dog will find the task a difficult one. Therefore, gradually increase the degree of difficulty over the course of about 20 repetitions (each about two minutes in duration). Usually, I do not try to do 20 repetitions in a row before going on to other things. Instead, do five to six reps until the dog and you can get around okay, then go on to other things. As we get into other commands, I will incorporate a short (two minute) session into future lessons, to make an exercise of about ten minutes in total. In addition, because this exercise is a difficult one, you will want to space this out by going back to Lesson 2 (walking in a straight line) as a means of relaxation.

The objective of Lesson 3 is to have your dog able to maintain the heel position as you change direction and speed at the walk. In order to avoid being stepped on, he must be prepared to react to each turn while staying in the correct position at all times. As in the previous lesson, your dog is expected to take the Sit position when you are stopped.

We can help the situation in two ways. First, by keeping the initial sessions fairly simple and then gradually making them more challenging. Second, we can provide cues – little signals that indicate when and which direction we are about to turn. This helps your dog maintain his position and hopefully avoid a bad fall on your part.

At first, your turns should be exaggerated and slow. The cues you give should be clear and also exaggerated. Eventually, the cues can be subtle and the speeds fast. Only you can determine when your dog is ready for the more difficult exercises. You should plan each exercise and based on what happened last time, add new wrinkles or review weak spots as required.

As usual, we will go through the process of lesson plan and lesson followed by review. In this section, I deal only with the first couple of repetitions. More repetitions will be incorporated into future lesson plans.

## I. Lesson Plan

The objective of this lesson is to first have your dog changing speeds to keep up with you and then changing directions as you execute fairly slow and easy to follow turns.

a) *Location.* Do your first session where the ground is level and easy to walk on. Likely, your previous location will do fine. Later, try walking to the store or some other location where there is some distraction.

b) *Length.* The total length of this session should still be about five minutes (juvenile) but this new material should only take two to three minutes of the total exercise. You should be prepared to fall back on the straight line work of the previous lesson, whenever things begin to feel a bit hectic. I often only do about 30 seconds of turns before going back to straight line for a minute or so.

c) *Plan.* Begin by doing some straight line work. Follow by changing speeds in a straight line. You should be able to go from your normal walking pace to a fast walk to a jog, with Heathcliff trotting in the heel position.

Since the left turn is easier for the dog heeling on the left side, start with the slow left turn (start with a right turn for the dog heeling on the right). Do two or three of these before doing a right turn. Execute two or three right and left combinations and then go back to the straight line work. Remember to have your dog sit when you stop. Give the correct cues and end your lesson earlier rather than later.

d) *Correction.* For the most part, corrections are soft, either gentle tugs on the leash or "Nooo."

The fear reaction should not be an issue at this point. Occasionally a juvenile will start to panic because things are happening too fast. If you are seeing this, slow down or take a short break to let him gather his wits.

Nor should there be any resistance to the program. Occasionally a dog will try to burst away, particularly when you first start to jog. Based on your experience, you should provide a strong leash correction only if you believe you are seeing defiance.

In most cases, you are providing correction – not punishment. You have to be quick to let your dog know when he is out of position but remember, this is more a development of a skill than a contest of wills. You two should begin to feel like a team.

e) *Voice.* As before, both positive endorsement and correction are easily and effectively given by voice. Anticipation is the key to being effective. This little game of "Where am I Going Next?" should be fun for both of you. Make your voice show that.

Eventually, you are going to remove the leash altogether. When that happens (not yet!), you will be entirely dependent on voice to direct and correct your dog. Start relying on your voice more and more from here on.

## II. Execute the Plan

Step 1. Review the previous work by having your dog heel on a straightaway. Do not vary your speed or turn. Stop frequently and have your dog sit in the correct position. You do not have to do this very long – perhaps 100 feet (30 metres) or so. Keep things positive and make sure your dog is doing things correctly before going on. If you get into a fight here, do not go on to the next step. Save that for another day.

Step 2. Still going in a straight line, begin to increase your speed. At first I pat my left leg with my left hand and make a clicking sound with my tongue to give lots of encouragement. These are your initial cues. As time goes by you can get to the point where you can signal a change of pace by moving your fingers in your left hand. This cue is so subtle that most observers do not notice it, but your dog will.

Vary your speed from normal to medium to fast, over the course to 200 feet (60 m) or so. Your dog will likely pick this skill up quickly. Especially if you consistently give him the cues!

Step 3. To execute the left turn, have your dog sitting on the left side in the correct position. Leading off with the left leg, take a couple of steps. Pivoting on your left foot, swing your right foot over to effect a 90° turn (¼ of a circle). You should exaggerate your movement to be like a goose-step. As you make your turn, click your tongue or repeat the heel command and then proceed in the new direction for a few feet.

> Note: If you have trained your dog to heel on the right, the process is the same except that you execute a right turn and the cues are off the right leg.

If your dog was in the correct position, he did not get stepped on. Instead, he was able to see that you planted your left foot for the pivot. Normally, you have been planting your left foot on the stop. Therefore, when you planted your left foot he began to stop, which helped him see the right leg coming over to make the turn. The click noise or the heel command repeated tells him that we are not going to stop and he can easily pick up the position as you proceed.

This turn is an inside turn for your dog and is much easier than the outside turn because he does not have to speed up to maintain his position. If he fails to recognize the left foot cue, he will not slow down and will likely get stepped on. Go ahead step on him . . . or at least make it a near miss. The fault is his – provided you have been stopping properly in the past. If not, the fault is yours . . . shape up!

Step 4. The right turn is a bit more difficult. As before, start off by leading with your left leg. After a few steps, plant your right foot and pivot. Bring your left leg around to make the right turn. Don't goose-step. Instead, slow down your turn so that your dog can follow your left foot through the turn. Step down on your left foot and continue for a few feet. Keep clicking and talking as you make your turn.

Step 5. Combine straightaway work with (two or three) right and left turns. Then do a series of speed changes. Do not try to put it all together right away. Make the transitions easy to follow. Keep this first session to no more than five minutes.

## Summary

This lesson and subsequent repetitions are a challenge to your dog. Start off fairly simply. Then begin to put movements, turns and speeds together so that it becomes more difficult. After a few repetitions, you should take your dog to the store or on a simple walk away from the normal training ground. Begin, also, to be more demanding in terms of making your turns crisp and abrupt. Make your cues more subtle. Do this lesson until you feel fairly comfortable getting around, then add the next lesson to your program, each time reviewing this lesson and refining your skills as you go.

A word or two about vocabulary – okay, and a story too. I have heard people say that a dog is capable of understanding a fairly significant number of words and phrases.

One book suggested that its author's dog understood over 1 200 words. Boy! That should qualify the dog for a few colleges I can think of – especially if he could carry a football.

I sold a neighbor of mine a young Border Collie bitch. We'll call this fellow Bill because that's his name. Bill is a local farmer, a delightful and thoroughly enjoyable character. The stories of his pranks and practical jokes would fill another book.

After an appropriate length of time Bill brought his bitch "Cuff" back to me for a little training. I dutifully began all the obedience work, which she picked up quite quickly. Then, I took her to herd some sheep and after about a month she got to be pretty useful. She was a bright, biddable and talented little dog – quite soft.

When Bill showed up, which he often did during this month of training, we would go out together and work Cuff. Bill would mostly watch and make small talk. When it came time to send Cuff home, I was keen to follow her progress since both she and Bill had learned most of the basic commands required to move stock around.

A month later I stopped by Bill's place for coffee. After a polite interval I asked to see Cuff work. Bill got up from the kitchen table and said to Cuff, "You know the heifers in the south field? Go bring em in." He opened the back door, let Cuff out and with a wink returned to the kitchen table where we resumed our coffee chat. After about ten minutes Cuffs showed up at the pens with half a dozen heifers.

I know a set-up when I see one and I strongly suspected that Bill and Cuff had done this exact routine every day for the last month. So I suggested I'd be interested in seeing Cuff do some *actual* work. We went out to the yard where the rest of the cattle are kept. Bill said to Cuff, "Bring em up – way around." Cuff started off in the wrong direction. Bill says "No! @$#%^." Cuff, without any hesitation, reversed direction. From there on, the session was basically Cuff trying to figure what Bill wanted and Bill indicating support with either "Ya" or "No . . . %^$_&&*&#@!" at which point Cuff would simply try the other thing.

Cuff and Bill always seemed to get the job done. After a few years of this, Cuff pretty well ran the place. If Bill wanted pigs loaded, he simply backed up the truck and told Cuff to load pigs. If she started on one he didn't want, he'd say so and in a matter of minutes it was all done. If you've ever tried to load pigs you will know just how incredible that story is. I was continually amazed by Cuff. Not so much by what she could do but how she figured out what Bill wanted and the vocabulary this dog appeared to have.

Sheep, cattle or pigs, it didn't matter to Cuff. She seemed to understand an amazing amount of what Bill said. His tone was usually conversational, punctuated with expletives. None of it fazed Cuff and most of it she seemed to understand. If she didn't know 1 200 words it was close and working with Bill, most of those were probably cuss words.

I don't know just how much vocabulary the average dog is capable of understanding but I will bet it is a lot more than you think. Rely on your voice to give your dog direction, correction and encouragement. The sooner you do this, the greater will be his eventual vocabulary and the more he will be able to do for you. Don't underestimate your dog like I did Cuff.

# Lesson 3
# Heel – "Vary Speeds and Direction"

## Schedule A: Juvenile Dogs

Copy this sheet and take it with you. Check off the items as they are completed.

_____ lesson plan completed

_____ location selected

_____ equipment checked

_____ maintained position during review "Sit on command"

_____ dog maintained position through variable speeds from walk to jog and back

_____ maintained position through slow left and right turn

_____ gave correction and praise correctly

_____ used your voice effectively

_____ lesson ended on a positive note and on time (five minutes)

*Note: This schedule is really just for the first four or five repetitions. You should be able to start doing faster turns, more demanding transitions and longer sessions (10 minutes) fairly soon now.*

*Remember, how fast you progress will depend on your dog. Age makes a great deal of difference at this point in time. Dogs from 6 to 8 months are likely to be slower in their abilities than even the slightly older ones. Do not push too hard.*

*Younger dogs tend to struggle with this skill more than the older ones do – be patient. Usually, when a young dog resists this exercise, it is because you are putting*

*too much new material in front of him. Short breaks in*
*your exercise should help.*

Question:     Did you see any evidence of fear during your
              lesson? Was there still some fear at the
              end of your lesson?

Clue:         Younger dogs will often show great concern
              (fear) when things start to happen too fast
              – slow down and do more reps. Make your
              sessions easier for the next two to three
              reps. Verbally encourage your dog!

Question:     Is there anything different that you would
              like to do next time? If so, make a note of
              it now.

# Lesson 3
# Heel – "Vary Speeds and Direction"

## Schedule B: Mature Dogs

Copy this sheet and take it with you. Check off the items as they are completed.

_____ lesson plan completed

_____ location selected

_____ equipment checked

_____ maintained position during review "Sit on command"

_____ dog maintained position through variable speeds from walk to jog and back

_____ maintained position through slow left and right turn

_____ gave correction and praise correctly

_____ used your voice effectively

_____ lesson ended on a positive note and on time (five minutes)

*Note: This schedule is really just for the first two or three repetitions. You should be able to start doing faster turns and more demanding transitions fairly soon now.*

*Remember, how fast you progress will depend on your dog. Age makes a great deal of difference at this point in time. Juveniles are likely to be slower in their abilities than even the slightly older ones. Because your dog is mentally more developed than the juveniles, you have a real advantage here. Even so, do not push too hard.*

*If your dog is showing signs of confusion, resistance or*

*fear, slow things down and treat him as more of a juve-
nile than a mature dog. Read the sections on juveniles.*

Question:     Did you see any evidence of fear during your
              lesson? Was there still some fear at the
              end of your lesson?

Clue:         While the older dogs tend not to be as over-
              whelmed by this exercise as the young
              ones, it happens occasionally. Make your
              sessions easier for the next two to three
              reps. Verbally encourage your dog!

Question:     Is there anything different that you would like
              to do next time? If so, make a note of it
              now.

# Lesson 4
# Any Speed, Any Direction

Over the years, I have had the pleasure of entertaining some of the top Border Collie handlers who come to Canada for stockdog competitions, usually from the US or the UK. They would stay over at my farm between trials.

One of the more enjoyable visits came when a woman from Arizona. "Dodie" stayed with us for a couple of weeks. She is still recognized as one of the best handlers in North America. During her stay, we trained our dogs in the morning and afternoon. In between, we talked about lesson plans for the next day. Early in this period, Dodie came in from a session with one of her dogs and announced that she had a great session with her dog because she finally got the "correction" she had been looking for.

For me, this was a different point of view. I usually do my training from the perspective of "what can we do right" and make corrections as I encounter them. Dodie, on the other hand, had set this lesson up from the perspective of "what can we do wrong," so that a particular flaw could be corrected.

I have since come to appreciate that a great deal can be accomplished by analyzing a flaw and setting up a correction. This lesson introduces you to a few flaws that you may be now dealing with and a few corrections that may be planned for.

If Lesson 3 can be considered the beginning of a skill, Lesson 4 should be considered the completion of that training. How many sessions or repetitions may be required to make this transition, is impossible to predict. Twenty sessions is not a bad estimate if the objective is to have your dog performing at a comfortable level of proficiency and yet that is probably not enough if you plan to compete in this area.

The mature dogs tend to come along faster than the juveniles once they get over arguing with you as to who is the boss. Part of this is, I think, because the older dogs can handle the pressure of a longer training session and because they have more life experiences to draw on than do the juveniles. Therefore, they actually receive more time on the task than do juveniles. Even so, mature dogs can be overloaded if you progress from one task to the next too quickly.

It is important that you do not let your dog get "slack" in his efforts to maintain the heel position as you go through your turns and speeds. This flaw can be easily corrected. In Lesson 3, you were encouraged to be positive and patient with your dog; to introduce new movements sequentially and not all at once. One of the results of your patient and positive approach is likely to be that your dog's position is more variable than it should be. Concentrate on allowing only the 6 inches (15 cm) of slack on the leash and no more. Practise making your turns exactly 90° and abrupt. If your dog starts to get ahead of you, do an immediate 180° turn to your right. Let the natural leash correction be fairly severe by not letting the leash pull through your hands. In fact, as you complete the turn, give the leash a sharp little jerk. If the dog is in the correct position, he will not feel anything but if he is the least bit behind, he will feel the correction.

At the conclusion of this lesson, your dog should be proficient at the heel. He should sit on command every time, without repeating the command. You both should enjoy the exercises and look upon them as a game. Most of the dogs I have trained to this point start to get cocky and seem to be saying, "It doesn't matter what you do. I bet you can't shake me."

## I. Lesson Plan

The objective of this lesson and series of exercises is to complete the heel training. Your dog should feel at ease going anywhere on the leash at any time. Positioning through any set of movements should be automatic. Commands need only be given once as he will be immune to distraction.

a) *Location.* For the intensive sessions where I want to improve this skill by testing my dog with sharp turns and abrupt changes of pace, I will normally use my old training ground as before. However, it is also time to start testing your dog with distraction and for that you need other people, traffic, other dogs and strange noises. A walk downtown during rush hour or in the park on a Sunday afternoon would do it. Use your imagination and vary your choice of location as often as possible.

b) *Length.* The length of your sessions also needs to become more variable. For walks downtown or in the park, 45 minutes is not out of line because I am assuming that a walk is just that and not an intensive training session. Intensive training still needs to be kept fairly short, 10 – 15 minutes for mature dogs and 10 minutes for juveniles is plenty, if you are requiring a high degree of performance during any part of the session.

c) *Plan.* You are actually going to be doing two different types of sessions for this lesson. The first is your typical intensive training session. As before, start with a bit of straight-line work followed by changing your pace from walk to jog and back. This should take perhaps two minutes. Then you will do a few left and right turns at a moderate to slow pace – another two minutes. At a brisk walk, do a series of tight square turns and about faces – two minutes. Follow this with turns and straight line work at the jog, one minute. Finally complete the session with a normal walk in a straight line to cool off – two or three minutes. Include stopping as part of this exercise, by abruptly halting at various times. Give the command to sit only once, followed almost immediately by pressure on the leash.

The second type of session is to expose your dog to distraction. Generally it is done at a normal walking pace and the turns, etc., are not so abrupt. Be diligent when it comes to correcting your dog for position faults. While the exercise itself is easier, the temptations to wander off and visit or lag behind to sniff that new aroma are much greater than before. You are looking for the opportunity to correct this kind of behavior with a sharp leash reprimand. Your dog must learn that when heeling, nothing else in the world matters except maintaining his position. Look for situations that expose your dog to new distractions. Test him constantly with temptation and correct him each and every time.

I do not want you to think that your best friend will never again know the joys of sniffing the disgusting things they seem to be so interested in. He will have his freedom time – just not when he is under the heel command!

d) *Correction*. As usual, correction generally consists of voice and leash corrections. The "Nooo" is your warning signal. A sharp jerk on the leash is the consequence of ignoring the warning.

As the dog gains proficiency at this skill, I tend to rely more on the leash correction because he knows where he is supposed to be and failure to be there should be immediately discouraged. I do not mean that leash correction should always be severe but it does need to be immediate. Pain, or least significant pain, should generally be reserved for those occasions where outright disobedience is encountered. In which case, we are talking about punishment.

During intensive sessions, when I am trying to improve my dog's performance, I use the leash almost constantly. The sharp turns and abrupt stops should be tightly guided with tugs on the leash so that the dog feels them every time he is out of position and does not feel them when he is in position – although he knows that he has little slack to work with.

Distraction is a somewhat different scenario. When a dog gives into the temptation to sniff that other dog (or whatever), I usually give a "Nooo" and a jerk on the leash. Of course I do not stop walking, so the result is a fairly strong correction. Generally, if he listened to the "Nooo" fast enough, he didn't feel much of a jerk on the leash. If he didn't listen to the "Nooo," his neck will probably hurt for a couple of seconds.

e) *Voice*. Do not forget to be positive throughout these sessions. Follow your corrections with immediate praise for being in the right place. Use the "Nooo" as required. Don't putz around trying to verbally convince your dog to do the right thing. At this stage of his training, the leash is your primary tool needed to get that really tight performance.

## II. Execute the Plan

Step 1. Start with a normal training session. At first, do some straight line work to get in the groove. About two minutes is enough. Remember to change your pace from walk to jog and back.

Step 2. Pick up the tempo with another couple of minutes of turns, stops and straight lines at an even pace. Remember to "Sit" during your stops.

Step 3. Increase the challenge with two minutes of the whole routine at a brisk walk and keep everything as tight as you can. You need to work on this a bit before going on to Step 4. If your dog gets confused or frightened because of the pace, slow things down for about 30 seconds, then go back to the faster pace. This is really hard for your dog and requires a great deal of concentration. If you struggle at first, don't be disappointed. If you only get a few seconds of this fast-paced routine completed, congratulate yourself. It comes a little at a time.

Step 4. Peak with about one minute of the routine at the jog. You will find that you cannot do the real tight turns. Let the turns be more of an arc than a 90° turn. When you first try this, be positive with your voice to keep your dog's confidence level up. Later, a few clicks should do the trick.

<u>Step 5</u>. Cool off with two to three minutes of easy walking. Wind down. Spend some time telling your dog how good he was.

<u>Step 6</u>. After you have achieved some proficiency at the above routine and before the whole exercise gets to be a bit boring, lead your dog unto temptation . . . find locations where he will have to deal with distraction. At a comfortable pace, have him heel through this area. Concentrate on correcting him every time he gives in to a distraction. Walk as if your dog were not there. Except for an occasional word of encouragement or a growl "Nooo" when required, pretend he is not at your heel when you make turns or stops at lights. You will find that he is able to take responsibility for maintaining his position without much guidance from you.

This session can be quite long and can often be worked into such daily routines as going to the corner store. Forty-five minutes is plenty of time for this session.

# Chapter Two Test: Heel

This is it! Don't worry if things don't go perfectly. No need to throw yourself off of a tall curb.

The idea here is to give you and your dog a check point against which to gauge your progress and an opportunity to congratulate yourself on a job well done – although you have probably already noticed that you feel good about taking your dog for a walk and a bit superior toward all those "others" who are being towed through the park by unruly pets. Enjoy this little exercise.

1. Complete your routine – steps 1 to 6. You may do this in two parts if you wish.

2. Have a friend watch your routine. They should mark down each time you give a voice or leash correction to your dog. Have them score each step separately. For example:

| Step | Number of Corrections | Voice/Leash |
|------|-----------------------|-------------|
| 1 | 2 | 1V/1L |
| 2 | 1 | 1L |
| 3 | 3 | 1V/2L |
| 4 | 1 | 1L |
| 5 | 0 | |
| 6 | 2 | 2L |

3. Count up the total number of corrections. If over the course of your routine, you gave less than 10 corrections (however minor), you pass. If you gave 10 or more, you should analyze where the greatest number of corrections occurred. From there you should have a pretty good idea of what needs work.

If your friend is at all keen on the idea, try to have them note exactly what the corrections were given for (e.g.)

sit, right turn, jog. This information will give you an even better idea of what to work on.

4. If you passed . . . put on your cap and gown, play "Pomp and Circumstance" on your ghetto blaster and proceed to the next chapter.

5. If you did not pass, save the champagne – we have work to do. Review what went wrong and try again after a few more practice sessions. Ask yourself if the flaws are as a result of lack of confidence or defiance, distraction or failure to give the proper cues. Plan your lessons to address what you perceive the problem to be and note if you are improving or getting worse.

6. At some point, all this testing stuff can get discouraging. If you are tired of the challenge, move on to the next chapter anyway. Perfection is highly overrated.

CHAPTER **3**

# Lie Down,
# Stay and Come

**Y**ou should be pleased with yourself and Marmaduke as well! Most of the hard work has been done.

1. You have established yourself as the leader.

2. You have taught your dog to give to the leash, listen to your voice commands and generally submit to your directions. Do you remember when you thought these things were impossible to achieve?

This chapter deals with an additional three commands designed to provide you with a dog that has all the basic behavioral skills you require in order to get along on a day-to-day basis. Of course, so far we have these skills only when we have Marmaduke on a leash. The off-leash work comes later. For now you have to get along as best you can.

One of the things you will have discovered if you tried it is the tremendous benefits associated with confinement. Even though your dog requires exercise, exercise in a confined area has likely afforded you with some measure of control and has certainly improved his attitude toward your training sessions. If you are not already a fan of confinement, give it a try – its never too late to start.

These commands, as well as the "Heel," are designed to be started on the leash. During the upcoming lessons, we will also be using the long line. The long line is about 40 – 60 feet (12 – 18 m) of cord intended to act as an extension of the leash. It allows you to train at a distance. Usually, 1/4" (.5 cm) nylon cord will do but because it burn your hands, you should be using gloves.

# Lesson 5
# Lie Down

The "Lie down" command is a natural progression from the "Sit" command. It is relatively easy to teach and nicely sets up the stay command. There are a variety of ways to introduce the lie down. I have my preference but there are a number of equally workable alternatives.

It is best to introduce the Lie down as part of your normal training routine. Therefore, let's review for a moment what the normal routine consists of and what your dog has learned to date.

- he has learned to maintain the heel position through a variety of paces, any direction and in the presence of distraction

- he has learned to respond to voice and leash direction and correction; he no longer resists or resents these corrections if/when given properly but seeks to respond correctly because he has learned strategies for achieving both approval and relief; he has learned a number of cues that enable him to avoid correction altogether

- he has come to accept that you are "running the show" and therefore, looks to you for leadership; he also recognizes that he is not the "boss dog" – you are and as a consequence, he probably seeks your approval and affection more often than he did before

- he has become accustomed to a training session that starts with review, graduates to more difficult tasks, peaks with the most difficult or new material and cools off with the easy skills; he has come to enjoy the challenge and the feeling of accomplishment associated with your approval and his success.

This regime allows you to introduce new material as you go along. Take a quick look at what the routine was for Lesson 4. By shortening each of the sections within that routine, you can find two minutes or so of time to add the lie down session and still stay within your 10 minute limit. By this time, the mature dog could certainly stand to go over the 10 minute limit. Probably 15 – 20 minutes is within his range of concentration. The juvenile should still be kept fairly short, although 12 – 15 minutes is likely within his range. If you feel the need to extend the sessions to these limits, try it few times. Watch your dog. If he begins to show signs of confusion or resentment, go back to the 10 minute limit.

### I. Lesson Plan

The objective of this lesson is to have your dog lie down on command. In my opinion, the Lie down also includes "Stay" because your dog should take and hold any command until such time as you release him by saying "okay" or "that'll do" or you give him a new command such as "Heel" or "Sit." The Stay command is essentially used when I want a dog to hold a command for an exceptionally long period of time. The Lie down command can be given anytime except when heeling at a walk or jog – you should stop before giving the Lie down.

a) *Location*. Your normal training ground will do fine. As you progress through these sessions, there is some merit to using different locations from time to time. The exposure to new situations is good for you and your dog – livens things up a bit. Also, new locations serve to reinforce the idea that obedience is a requirement wherever you are and that is worth doing from time to time.

b) *Length*. You are going to work the Lie down, Stay and Come exercises into your old routine so that the overall length will stay about the same (10 – 15 minutes). The amount of time you will actually be practising lie down is about two minutes. You will find that the 10-minute rule is not so important now. The key to judging when to quit, is to watch your dog. If you notice him showing signs of confusion or resistance near the end of your sessions, you are probably not stopping soon enough. Be sensitive to the body language of your dog. When he shows signs of fatigue, stop the exercise.

c) *Plan*. The lesson should start with the same old routine; a bit of straight line work, some turns, stops and changes of pace. Take the real intensive fast-paced work out of your routine for now. During the course of walking at the heel, stop occasionally. When you do, command your dog to "Lie down." Take your left foot and step on the leash such that the dog's head is forced to the ground (see Figure 3a). Have the leash under your foot so that the leash is in front of the heel of your shoe. While you are standing on it, you can shorten or lengthen the leash as required (see Figure 3b). Take enough of the leash away from the dog so that the only comfortable position for him is lying down. Once he is settled into the position, give him another 20 seconds or so to take it all in. After you have done this a few times, remove your foot from the leash. If he starts to get up, you can either correct him with a "Nooo" or step back on the leash. Then walk off at the heel. Remember to give the "Heel" command and lead off with the left foot.

Do this exercise at least 10 times during your first session. Do not ask your dog to lie down every time you stop or he will anticipate the command and lie down before you ask him to. If he starts to do this, it can be corrected by stopping and starting again almost immediately, like a "touch and go" exercise that pilots do when they are learning to land an airplane. Another alternative is to give the sit command and require him to sit up.

As you progress on to other sessions, practise the command at oddball times and keep your dog down for longer periods of time. Also, you should add the fast paced heel work back into your program for short durations (one – two minutes). Finally, the Lie down needs to be done with distraction, although the true test for distraction is the stay command.

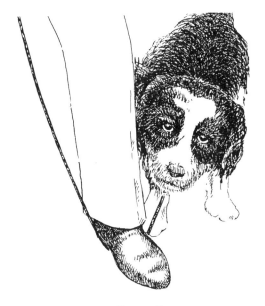

*Figure 3a*

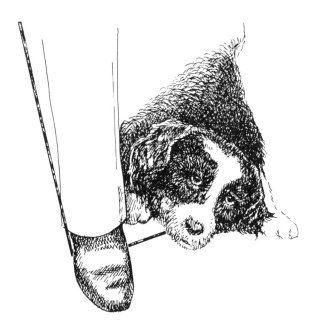

*Figure 3b*

d) *Correction.* At first, you will use the leash to put him in the correct position. Once there he will remain comfortable only as long as he stays down. Efforts to get up are automatically corrected by the leash because there is not enough leash slack to permit him to stand. Later, ask him to lie down and give him a couple of seconds to obey, after which either step on the leash or growl at him.

Often, at this point I take away just enough leash to make him uncomfortable but still able to stand or sit if he chooses. This is what I consider to be a very soft correction. I will leave him in this awkward position for quite some time with no further commands or correction. This appears to be especially useful for dogs that are prone to a fear reaction, because the mild discomfort allows them to make the decision after having time to think about it. I won't do this every time nor very long into the lesson, but early in the game it has its place.

e) *Voice.* As usual, the negative growl "Nooo" serves as a mild correction and normally does the trick. The more severe leash correction can be administered either severely, by stepping on the leash quickly and taking all the leash away or more gradually by either stepping on it slowly or by taking less on the leash away. Regardless, when you use the leash to correct, you should also be using your voice to enforce the command.

The positive side of this tool is the same as the Heel. The difference may be that when you say "good dog," he might try to get up, thinking he has been released. You should use "okay" or "that'll do" to release your dog from a command. The "good dog" can then be used solely for encouragement and to let him know he is doing the right thing.

Another voice command I use is "there." For the most part I use it when training stockdogs. It lets them know when they are in the right position relative to the cattle. This command is usually followed by another such as "Lie down" or "Get up." This is a bit like when someone is scratching your back and they finally get the right spot!

The point is that "good dog" is not the only positive thing you can say and it should not be used as a catch-all.

## II. Execute the Plan

Step 1. Start with straight line work. Walk about 75 – 100 feet (23 – 30 m) at the heel. Stop, allow about three seconds to get things settled. Bring enough slack through your left hand to allow you to step on the leash with your left foot. Command "Lie down" and at the same time, step on the leash. Pull the slack through the space in front of the heel of your shoe or have less slack to start with. Either way, this motion should pull your dog's head to within three inches (8 cm) of the ground. Do this movement with conviction – not forcefully but don't putz with it. Remember, he doesn't have any idea what you are talking about. Once your dog is in the correct position, say "There! Good dog!" Leave him in this position for 20 – 30 seconds. Leading off with your left foot, command "Heel" and start away at the walk. Leading off with the left foot automatically takes your foot off the leash. Don't lead off too quickly; allow him a bit of time to get up and start walking with you.

Step 2. Walk another 100 feet (30 m) at a leisurely pace. Stop and repeat the exercise. Start off at the walk again. For the next one to two minutes go through your normal routine without asking him to lie down. Complete a number of turns and ask him to sit a few times – keep things fairly easy.

Step 3. Repeat the Down exercise two or three times in a row. Walk for a bit, command "Lie down," then walk for a bit more. On the third time, ask him to lie down and allow three to five seconds for him to think about it. If he does not lie down, growl "Nooo" and forcefully step on the leash.

Step 4. Allow one to two minutes of normal exercise to intervene and then repeat Step 3. If you think you are seeing a fear reaction, try taking just a bit of the leash away, as we discussed in the "Correction" section of this lesson on the previous page. You should not see a great deal of resistance to this exercise. If you do, I suggest you have your dog examined by a vet for hip dysplasia because I have noticed that dogs with hip dysplasia sometimes have a difficult time with this exercise. If you are sure there is no medical reason for his reluctance, use a more severe leash correction by quickly stepping on the leash when you give the command. Do it immediately following the command and do it forcefully. Offer no slack and no praise for the first three to four times. Once he is taking the command without resistance and immediately, you positively reinforce his obedience.

Step 5. You should expect to do this lesson three to four times by which time your dog should be fairly consistent in his response. Try a final session in an area where there is some distraction. Assuming that is successful, the remainder of your repetitions should be incorporated into your future routines and interspersed with new commands.

Finally, you should begin to wean yourself off the leash. If/when your dog tries to get up before you are ready, use your voice (Nooo) to keep him in the down position before you step on the leash.

## Summary

While this exercise is generally fairly easy, there are occasionally a few minor problems. The first is when your dog is told to "Lie down," he may roll over and show his belly. This is a submission movement and is more common in juvenile, soft dogs. If you see this happening at this stage of your training you have a bigger problem than just the Lie down. A young dog can easily lose confidence in himself and in you. In my opinion, if a dog is still submitting after all this time, he has either lost confidence or for some reason, has become fearful of the process. The most common cause of this is being too severe with the leash and not giving enough verbal encouragement – more the latter than the former. Pump up your dog. Tell him when things are going well, even if you have to exaggerate once in a while. Work on his confidence and you will find that the rollovers will become less common. Once you have regained his enthusiasm, try stop, lie down and walk off, all in rapid succession. Basically, you have not given him time to rollover before you began walking again. A few of these "touch and go's" and he will give up trying to submit. Remember that the root of the problem was confidence and act accordingly in the future.

Another problem is persistent reluctance to take the command. Assuming that you have established there is no medical reason behind this behavior, you have likely tried the severe leash correction noted earlier. Occasionally, even that doesn't work in that your dog is waiting for the punishment every time before going down. In this case, try the mild leash correction, where you take only enough leash away to make him uncomfortable. He is standing or sitting with his head pulled half way to the ground – not forced to lie down but not comfortable anywhere else. Leave him in this position for four to five minutes if necessary. Usually, he will think about the situation for a while and then decide that down is easier than up. When he does this, congratulate him on the correctness of his thinking. Praise him with your voice and even give him a pat on the head. Leave him down for another two to three minutes.

Sometimes, the mild leash correction results in a fight. Your dog has stood there for a few seconds, thinking about his situation, and decided that fighting is the correct course of action. Shift your weight to your left foot and let him go at it. Don't get mad – get even. Let him hurt himself for a while and when he finds that this plan didn't work very well he will reconsider his options. Eventually, he will decide to lie down . . . although it may be midnight and you might be very tired.

Juveniles are sometimes so full of energy that the Lie down is almost more than they can bear. Young dogs often struggle with both the Down and Stay positions. You can make life a bit easier on both of you if you leave the Lie down work until later in your program. For exuberant dogs, I often give them the whole eight to ten minutes of routine (including two to three minutes of fast work) before I ask them to Lie down. By that time we are both a bit winded and the opportunity to lie down for a few seconds is welcome.

As you go on to other lessons, remember that periodic review of skills learned in the past is the norm. Incorporate this command into your routine and try to get three to four Lie downs into every session.

# Lesson 5
# Lie Down

## Schedule A: Juvenile Dogs

Copy this sheet and take it with you. Check off the items as they are completed.

\_\_\_\_\_ lesson plan completed

\_\_\_\_\_ location selected

\_\_\_\_\_ equipment checked

\_\_\_\_\_ review previous skills

\_\_\_\_\_ lie down successfully completed . . . 10 times

\_\_\_\_\_ length of time left down was varied from 10 seconds to 1 minute

\_\_\_\_\_ the Lie down command was given under a variety of situations and locations

\_\_\_\_\_ leash and voice corrections given properly

\_\_\_\_\_ voice praise given freely

\_\_\_\_\_ repeat this lesson at least three times before going to Lesson 6

\_\_\_\_\_ incorporate the Lie down command into future lessons

# Lesson 5
# Lie Down

## Schedule B: Mature Dogs

Copy this sheet and take it with you. Check off the items as they are completed.

_____ lesson plan completed

_____ location selected

_____ equipment checked

_____ review previous skills

_____ lie down successfully completed . . . 10 times

_____ length of time left down was varied from 10 seconds to 1 minute

_____ the Lie down command was given under a variety of situations and locations

_____ leash and voice corrections given properly

_____ voice praise given freely

_____ repeat this lesson at least two times before going to Lesson 6

_____ incorporate the Lie down command into future lessons

# Lesson 6

# Stay

_____

The Stay command is perhaps the most often abused and therefore, inconsistent command, used by the beginning trainer. I think the reason for this is because there is a tendency to forget to release your dog and a further tendency to ask your dog to stay for totally unreasonable lengths of time. For example, I have seen people tie their dog in front of the market, issue a stern "Stay" command and proceed to go shopping for a hour or so. What strikes me about this, is that the dog is tied up – he's not going anywhere – so why tell him to stay in the first place? Secondly, the owner has no intention of enforcing the command since he doesn't plan to be around for the next hour or so. If he doesn't routinely enforce the command, why give it?

The stay is an exercise in discipline for you and your dog. You should expect to build this skill gradually, by first asking and enforcing a stay over a short period of time and with no distraction. Later, you will need to add both distraction and length to your expectations. Other than to prove a point, I would rarely ask a dog to stay more than five minutes. Generally, if I am going to be away longer, I will kennel or tie the dog. To me, it just makes sense.

The Stay command should be used sparingly and only when you need it. Otherwise, your dog will begin to treat the command as an optional exercise.

I recall a hunting trip one sunny September afternoon. My hunting partner and I were cruising the ditches looking for Hungarian Partridge. Al is a big guy, about 6' 4" and about 240 pounds. He is a pretty good gundog trainer in his own right. Over the years we have spent many happy hours arguing about the relative merits of dogs, breeds and training techniques. You see, Al likes his Labradors and he is of the general opinion that Border Collies are basically sissies.

It was during one of these conversations, in which Al was extolling the virtues of Labs and allowing as how they were more obedient because they had superior powers of concentration, that we came upon a flock of 20 or so "Huns." Tigger was a big, tough (and I thought, somewhat stupid) black Lab. Tigger was the object of Al's latest affection. I liked Tigger too. Tigger would find Huns or grouse and ducks. Most importantly, Tigger would bring ducks out of the slough in the autumn. In Alberta, water in Autumn is always cold, if it isn't already stiff. So the fact that Tigger was willing to break ice all day to retrieve the ducks we shot, made Tigger okay with me.

*"Tigger"*

The Huns busted out in a flurry. It seemed they filled the sky in an instant. I brought down one, Al brought down two. As I bent down to pick up my shell, I could see the Huns land about 100 yards away. So did Al . . . so did Tigger. Like Mighty Casey at the Bat, Al ordered Tigger to "LIE DOWN" and for insurance said "STAY." We knew Tigger was a rock.

Al and I spread out and started to where we saw the Huns land. As we walked through the stubble we stepped over the swaths of barley carefully. Within a couple of minutes, we were getting close. They should be in there somewhere . . . all at once, this low-slung bundle of muscle and hair streaked past my feet, ploughing a swath into the Hun patch. Out of range now, the Huns circled above our heads and took leave of our company.

Al was not amused. With a roar that would do a bull elephant proud, Al hollered "Tigger @#$$!! and LIE DOWN you $@^&!!" So far, Tigger had been running wildly about until it dawned on him that perhaps that wasn't the smartest decision he'd ever made and perhaps he should make like the Huns. The next half hour or so constituted one of the most enjoyable hunting trips I've ever had. I sat down on a rock and watched Al chase Tigger up and down that barley field into the setting harvest sun. I learned words my mother never taught me. I watched blood pressure rise to new medical highs as Tigger carefully kept 20 feet away from sure death. I laughed so much that I thought Al would kill me before he got around to Tigger. I was reminded that even very good dogs will break a stay command and make a liar out of you in a second.

The Stay command is something that requires regular reinforcement throughout your dog's life. Occasional reminders are needed. By the way, Tigger was **very** good for a long time after that day.

The "Stay" command means "don't move." To be precise, your dog should not shift or change positions and certainly not wander off. If you just want your dog to wait in the back of the truck and bite anybody that tries to steal your tools, you should not be using Stay. Try using "wait here" instead. If you mean "don't move," you must be prepared to enforce it and you should have a means of releasing when finished, such as "okay." I think the Stay command is worth doing properly. It needs to be practised at a distance as well as at hand. Therefore, in addition to our normal set of tools, we will be using a long line. We will ask the dog to stay and correct him even from fairly long distances. We will not permit him to change from Sit to Lie down, nor will he be permitted to change locations from where we put him.

## I. Lesson Plan

There are a couple of ways to approach this lesson. The first is to introduce the Stay from the Lie down position. The second way is to do it from the sit position. If you are thinking of going on to obedience competition, you should probably start with the sit. The reason for this is because your dog will hold the Sit-Stay command better if you start with it. On the other hand, the Lie down is an effective way to begin because it is a bit easier to keep a dog in place from the Lie down. Personally, I very seldom use the Sit-Stay command. Most of the time, if I want a dog to stay, I'll ask him to Lie down first. We will cover both combinations.

At this point, you have practised both the Sit and Lie down commands extensively. Your dog is steady on both. As part of your routine, you can add a slight variation by holding the Stay and Lie down a little longer than normal. Try to extend each of these commands to about 30 seconds while on leash, as part of your Heel pattern. Vary the duration of Sit and Lie down, each time you do it.

Once you are sure your dog will not anticipate the Heel command immediately after the Sit or Lie down, you can practise stepping a few feet away from your dog while leaving him in position. Later we will extend the distance by using the long line. Finally, we will practise this command in the presence of distraction.

## II. Execute the Plan

Step 1. Using your quiet training ground, go through your standard training routine. Practise your Heel, turns, changes of pace for a few minutes. It is best to take some of the air out of your dog before asking him to "Stay" as he will be more inclined to accept this command. When you stop, ask your dog to "Sit." Under normal circumstances, you have probably only been stopping for a few seconds.

This time, wait for at least 10 seconds before resuming the Heel exercise. If your dog starts to get up, apply the leash correction and a low growl and make him wait a bit longer. Repeat this exercise at least three times, adding 10 seconds on to the wait period each time. Do not ask him to Stay. The point of this exercise is to make sure your dog is not anticipating the Heel command before you are ready. Remember not to shift your feet around as he may take this as a cue.

Step 2. Repeat the exercise in Step 1, incorporating the Lie down. Alternate, if possible, the Sit and the Lie down each time you stop. Now your dog has almost no chance to anticipate commands and must wait for your signal. At the conclusion of these exercises, you should be about eight minutes into your routine.

Step 3. You can have your dog do this exercise either from the Sit or the Lie down position. I prefer the Lie down because I find it easier to keep a dog down than to maintain a sit. Once you give the Stay command, you do not want your dog to change position. If you started from the sit and your dog lies down, correct him by returning him to the Sit position with a leash correction. This happens quite often with young dogs because the Lie down is more comfortable. When it does happen you are presented with the dilemma of correcting the Sit command and possibly confusing your dog with respect to the Stay command.

Now that I have thoroughly confused the issue, you decide – Sit or Lie down. Assuming that you choose Lie down as your starting point, the next time you come to a stop in your routine, ask your dog to Lie down. Put your left foot on the leash, as you did when you first started this command. Once he is down, bring your *right* hand down in front of the dog's nose (palm open). At the same time issue a firm "Stay" command and take one step with your *right* foot. Leave your left foot on the leash. Slowly bring your left foot away from the leash, pivot and bring your left foot (take your foot off the leash) beside your right foot, facing your dog (see Figures 4a – 4c, next page). Hold this position for about 10 seconds and then return to your dog's

*Figure 4a*

*Figure 4b*

*Figure 4c*

side, facing the same direction as your dog and ready for the Heel command. Give the Heel command and lead off with the left foot.

If your dog moves while you are facing him, give a sharp "Nooo" and quickly put your left foot back on the leash. Repeat this exercise several times until your dog is steady and waits, in position, for your Heel command at the end. Each time you do this exercise, keep your dog down a little longer so that by the end, he will hold the Down position for about a minute.

Step 4. Take a long piece of rope and attach it to the end of your leash. Now try the Down command. Don't feel that you have to go through the whole Heel exercise. Your dog should take the Down command fairly quickly at any time. Tell him to "Stay" and, leading off with the right foot, back away from him 6 – 10 feet. Return to his side after about 10 seconds. Repeat this exercise at least 10 times. Each time vary the distance away from your dog and the length of time you ask him to stay. If you have 40 feet (12 m) of cord, you should try to get to the end of the cord on at least one occasion before moving on to the next lesson.

Step 5. You may wish to do this exercise on a different day. Take your dog to a park or some place where there is a lot of distraction. Other dogs, other people (especially children) and strange noises are all distractions. Repeat Steps 1 to 4. Be prepared to do a lot of correction. If you are strict during the early part of this lesson you shouldn't have a great deal of trouble when you get to the long line. However, if you do, go back to the short work for the rest of the day. Leave the long line work for another day. Also, take note of which distractions caused you the most trouble and try to expose your dog to those distractions more often.

## Summary

The juvenile dog usually has the most problem with this skill. The soft dogs often completely collapse when given the Down command, especially the juveniles. Sometimes they crawl on their bellies and/or roll over. As usual, a lot of positive encouragement is required. However, many dogs insist on getting up or coming to you every time you offer encouragement. This can be quite frustrating.

Figure 5 illustrates a handy method for preventing the "belly crawl." Simply attach one end of your cord to the dog's collar, slip the other end around a post and back to the dog's collar. Now you have both forward and backward control by taking a position along the loop. If your dog tries to belly crawl up to you, apply a leash correction by pulling on the cord so that it pulls him back into position. If he tries to run away, simply correct by pulling on the other part of the line.

*Figure 5*

A similar device can be set up for the dog that habitually lies down following a Sit command. Loop your cord over some sort of cross bar and tell him to sit beneath it. If he tries to lie down as you back away, you can pull on the cord to lift him up again. Remember, this isn't a hanging at high noon but rather a leash correction – a few quick jerks is sufficient. This rope trick works on all ages of dogs but is more effective on the juveniles.

Juveniles frequently have an overabundance of energy. It is usually best to exercise your dog *before* trying the Stay command. For the youngsters, staying in one place for any length of time is difficult. It is best to tire them out first, if you can.

The mature dogs don't have nearly as much trouble with the Stay. The problem with the older ones is that they are too smart. They have learned that unless you are right there they probably won't get caught if they move. It may take some additional work and perhaps some devious planning to get them to change their minds on this matter. The long line is useful for extending the range at which your dog will listen. Other strategies include hiding behind the corner of a building or car. I have even gone so far as to get in my car and drive away while I had a friend watch my dog and correct with the long line if he broke – unfair but effective. Some folks even go to the extent of using electric dog collars. They can be extremely effective if used properly, but it takes a lot of experience to know exactly when to apply the correction.

It is much less common for a dog to sit up while being told "Stay" in the down position. However, it does happen from time to time. If your dog sits up, you should correct this immediately. The Stay means "don't move from your last position" and if you allow him to sit up, it won't be long before he is walking around. Also, if you ever plan to go into obedience competition, this seemingly minor flaw will cost you any chance at a ribbon, even at the junior level. Most dogs will think about sitting up for a few seconds before they actually do. You can see them lift up their heads, look around and slowly start to rise on their front feet. A growled "Nooo" will usually correct this before he actually gets up. If you are too late for that, step on the leash and quickly force him back into position.

At some point, most dogs just have to try to get away. Usually, this happens with a distraction while doing the off-leash work. Once a dog is gone it proves nothing to be calling and cooing to him. In fact quite the opposite; he will quickly understand you can't catch him. The reason I mention this now, is that this is the first lesson where the possibility of escape is at all likely during a training session. The only thing I have found to be really effective (outside of the electric collar) is to walk the dog down. I don't call to him. I don't scold him. I just walk to him.

Eventually, the pressure of being hunted becomes too much for him and he will either run to his home or lie down and submit. When I catch him, I will grab his nose and squeeze, growl, pick him up by the collar (if I can), shake him hard and put him back on the ground and stand over him. Sometimes I have walked for nearly an hour to catch a dog this way. I can remember only one dog that ran from me for more than that. Usually, it takes less than half an hour.

Now, if your dog should happen to break away while he is on the long line you have a tremendous advantage. Catching him again should be fairly easy but I suggest you don't catch him too quickly. Instead, let him think for a few minutes that he has really put one over on you. Walk toward him and let him make the decision to run. If he doesn't, fine but if he does – let him commit fully to the escape. Once he has fully committed, you should be able to catch him within a few minutes. Remember, don't call to him – just keep walking after him. When you get the chance, step on the long line and give it your best jerk. Walk the rest of the way to him and give him the strongest correction you can muster. If you do this at this stage of training, you may not have to do it later.

The Stay command is an acquired skill. It takes practice in front of distractions of all kinds and just because your dog will hold a stay for five minutes does not mean he is good for ten or even six minutes. The best rule of thumb is, never ask your dog to Stay unsupervised longer than you have already done in practice. If you introduce "Wait here" as an alternative to "Stay," for those times when you are going to leave him in the car or tied to a post, you will find it much easier to maintain the Stay.

You should plan on repeating this lesson only two or three times before moving on to the "Come here" lesson. I don't think that you have to practice "Stay" until your dog holds this position overnight. If he is pretty good up to one minute, move on. The Stay command is complementary to the Come here command. Practice sessions that include "Down," "Stay" and "Come" go well together. Therefore, as you practise "Come here", you will find that "Stay" also improves and that you can do it without boring either your dog or yourself.

Finally, I have combined the Training Summary Schedule for both the juvenile and the mature dog into one. The reason for this is because the two are close now in terms of their training and, for the most part, their reaction to the introduction of new material. Other than the fact that mature dogs tend to be a little cagier and juveniles still tend to panic a bit at times, the approach is essentially the same. The length of time you can train is still shorter for the juvenile, but the difference should be minimal. Also, by now, you have developed a feel for your dog – a sense of rapport that allows you to know what he is thinking and what his reaction to various situations is likely to be. As the distinction between juvenile and mature becomes somewhat less important, you have learned a lot as well and are able to focus on your dog as an individual as opposed to a category. You are in a position to take considerable liberties with lesson plans, based on what you know about your dog and in doing so, make them more effective.

# Lesson 6
## Stay

———

### Juvenile and Mature Dogs

Copy this sheet and take it with you. Check off the items as they are completed.

\_\_\_\_\_ lesson plan completed

\_\_\_\_\_ two locations selected (with and without distraction)

\_\_\_\_\_ equipment checked (add long line & gloves)

\_\_\_\_\_ review previous skills

\_\_\_\_\_ Stay command completed on leash from both Down and Sit positions

\_\_\_\_\_ Stay command successfully completed at least 10 times and for at least 1 minute.

\_\_\_\_\_ Stay command completed on long line (with and without distraction)

\_\_\_\_\_ leash and voice corrections given properly

\_\_\_\_\_ voice praise given freely

\_\_\_\_\_ repeat this lesson at least two times with distraction

\_\_\_\_\_ incorporate this command into future lessons

\_\_\_\_\_ overall training time should be 15 – 20 minutes per session

# Lesson 7
# Come

Here it is, after all this time – what you wanted in the first place – a dog that will come when called. I did not wait until the seventh lesson to talk about this out of some sort of sadistic master plan, nor did you learn all that other stuff just for the heck of it. In fact, what you and your dog have learned so far has been a necessary prerequisite to this command because it requires that you be firmly "in the driver's seat" before your dog will consistently obey a "Come here" command. Waiting this long to introduce this command makes it a relatively easy and quickly learned skill on the part of your dog.

Much of the work for this lesson will be done on the long line. We want to approximate the off-leash work without losing control of the dog since the "Come here" command is of little practical use when the dog is on a leash. As much as possible, I like to let the dog think he has more freedom than he really does. Therefore, after I have completed a relatively brief amount of practice on the standard leash, I will tie the long line to the collar and increase the distance from which I call him. At the conclusion of this lesson, I like to let the dog run free for a little distance, perhaps letting him drag the long line behind him as he runs around. From time to time I call him to come, knowing that I can quickly step on the long line if need be.

Like any other skill, the "Come here" command is one that is gained gradually. Unlike some of the others, this command is learned quickly. Therefore, it can easily be incorporated into your routine. For instance, within a typical routine, I might take three or four minutes to practise Come, Lie down and Stay by putting my dog

Down-Stay and walk to the end of my long line (40 – 60 feet, or 12 – 18 m). After a comfortable period, I call my dog to come. Before he gets halfway, I tell him to "Lie down," then "Come," then "Lie down–Stay," then "Come" and so on. A great variety of sequences can be used in a short period and the incorporation of this command with the others actually strengthens "Come here."

One of the reasons why "Come here" is often perceived as a difficult command to master is because there is a tendency to use it only in emergencies. Under normal circumstances, your dog is coming up to you all the time; either for attention or food or whatever. If you only call your dog to "Come here" when he is distracted by something and wants to leave, then it is little wonder that you have a problem. Now . . . I know you would never do such a thing, but I confess, I have a tendency to do it. Therefore, I have to practise the "Come here" at times when I have no reason, so that he will come when I need him to.

### I. Lesson Plan

Start with your normal routine. By now you could probably drop the simple things like straight line work at heel. If fact the whole Heel session could probably be reduced to a couple of minutes since your dog is likely getting a fair amount of practice just walking to the store or other daily routines. You should spend two to three minutes reviewing the variable speeds and more difficult turns; partly to sharpen up your dog but also to take a bit of the edge off him before going on to "Lie down," "Stay" and "Come here" commands.

Using the short leash, practise "Lie down" two or three times in a row. Practise "Stay" another two or three times for intervals of up to 30 seconds, to make sure he remembers everything. So far, during the Stay command, you have put your dog in either the "Sit" or "Lie down" position, placing your hand in front of his nose, ordered "Stay" and walked (right foot) to the end of the leash. After a decent interval, you have returned to his side and either said "Okay" or "Heel," depending on what you were about to do next. This time, do everything the same except that when you have waited 10 – 20 seconds, tell him to "Come here," followed immediately by a light tug on the leash. Your dog should come immediately up to your feet so that you are facing each other. With your right hand on the leash so that he is pulled to your right-hand side, tell him to "Finish" and give him another tug. Continue to direct him around behind you and into the heel position on your left-hand side. Then walk away at the heel, after giving the heel command. Remember which foot to lead off with.

I like my dogs to come to me and sit facing me. Many dogs seem to do this automatically. When a dog comes on a recall and stops, facing me, I will usually have him sit for a few seconds before asking him to "finish." Of course, this is up to you, but I like it. It looks sharp, adds even further control and I think, helps prevent dogs from jumping up on you.

Complete this exercise several times. It is important to mix things up a bit so that he doesn't start to move before you give the command. Therefore, about every second or third time, don't call "Come here." Instead, walk back to him as you did in the previous lesson. Also, don't always ask him to "Finish." From time to time, it is useful to go directly from "Come" to "Sit-Stay" and repeat the walk away. Use your own judgment; the point is that you do not want him to come to you every time you twitch and you do not always want him to "Finish" as you may decide to do something other than heel following "Come."

Once you feel things are under control on the short leash, attach the long line and repeat the exercise a few more times. Since you have the long line, you have the option of stopping your dog at various points during a recall ("Come here") by saying "Sit" or "Lie down." You can add further variations to the program by occasionally stopping a recall and walking up to him instead of having him come to you all the way. The objective is to have a dog that not only will come when he is called, but will stop and take other directions along the way. When you want to stop your dog before he gets to you, try (at least at first) throwing your hand out in a halt gesture and take a half step toward him as you say "Sit" or "Lie down." Follow this with a "Nooo" if he doesn't listen right away.

Finally, this exercise should be repeated at least once with distraction. Again, choose your park, or whatever, to expose your dog to other people, sounds and dogs to be sure that in fact you have control.

## II. Execute the Plan

<u>Step 1</u>. Start with a couple of minutes of review. Do a few quick turns and perhaps some jogging at the Heel. Practise Sit, Lie down and Stay on the short line. Mix things up a bit so that Marmaduke is "on the ball."

<u>Step 2.</u> Have your dog Sit-Stay. Back up to the end of your leash. Say, "Marmaduke, come here." Immediately follow this with a couple of light tugs on the leash. If he stops along the way, give another tug but don't repeat the command. When he gets to you, facing you, tell him to "Sit." Allow 5-10 seconds and command "Finish." Take the leash in your right hand and tug him to your right and behind you. Repeat the command and tug him into the heel position. Praise your dog. Walk for 20 to 30 feet (6 to 9 m) at the heel.

If you have any problems with this step, try reading Lesson 1 – Basic Leash Work, again. It may give you some ideas. Normally, you shouldn't have much trouble unless your dog decides to resist out of a sense of defiance. In this case, try changing your "tug" to a "jerk" and be a bit more demanding about the whole thing.

<u>Step 3</u>. Repeat Step 2 at least three times. Ask your dog to both "Sit" and "Finish" each time. On the fourth time, have him sit and tell him to "Stay." Back away and tell him "Come here." Do this twice without the finish and finish on the third time. Complete this step with a short walk at the heel. Give him a minute or so of easy walking to relax.

<u>Step 4</u>. Attach the long line and repeat Step 3. This time back 20 or 30 feet away before recalling your dog. With each repetition, back a little further away from your dog until you are at the end of the line. You will notice that

Step 3 included six recalls with some variations. On the sixth recall on the long line, stop your dog about half way to you by commanding "Lie down." Put your hand out in a halting gesture and if necessary, take one or two steps toward him. It is important that he take the Lie down as quickly as possible. Leave him down for 10 – 20 seconds and then recall him the rest of the way.

Step 5. Make a game out of the recall on the long line by stopping your dog several times along the way with sit or lie down. Vary the amount of time you leave him in position before recalling. From time to time, recall him all the way without stopping. Make it sort of like the children's game "Red Light, Green Light." Most dogs really like this game and can do it for several minutes without feeling any great deal of stress. However, if you see that your dog is not enjoying the exercise, stop for today. Either way, you probably shouldn't do more than two to three minutes of this.

Step 6. Without taking a great deal of time and repetitions, you should do a little practice with distraction. Select a location with lots of interesting things for your dog. Repeat Step 5 a few times. Leave him in the stay position for one to two minutes and give him an opportunity to break away. If he does, correct him and repeat the exercise. If he does not break, call it a day.

## Summary

Your dog should be steady on the long line for all of the commands given thus far. He should stay for periods that seem to you reasonable. I suggest two to three minutes is plenty but you can certainly go longer if you wish. He should sit, lie down and come, willingly and without repeating the command.

The most common problem encountered with this lesson is in Step 4. Juvenile dogs in particular often have a problem with switching commands. Once they are into the "Come here" mode you find you can't get them stopped until they have completed "Come here." The easiest way to correct this problem is to use your long line around a post, like we did for Lesson 6 – Stay (see Figure 5 on p. 96). You might want to get a longer line since the loop effectively halves the length of your line.

Take your long line and attach one end to your dog's collar. Feed the other end around a post or similar device and back to your dog's collar. Once both ends are attached, you have made a circuit with your line. Put your dog in a Stay position and go as far away from the post as you can. Letting the line run through your hand, recall your dog. To stop him at any time, simply close your hand on the cord. Remember to give your dog both the voice command and the hand cues before stopping him with the line. At first, I make the delay quite noticeable. But after only a couple of times, I will stop him with the line almost at the same time as I give the command. This makes for a dog that will stop in a hurry so don't do this on pavement or somewhere where he can hurt himself. If your dog refuses to lie down or sit while on the line, give it a jerk and repeat the command (once only). Don't get in the habit of doing this as it will encourage your dog to wait for the command twice – not a good plan.

While I'm on the subject of repeating commands: I often repeat a new command, perhaps several times. I continue to repeat commands if I think it is doing some good. I believe soft dogs need to have commands repeated in the early going, in much the same way as they need positive reinforcement when they attempt tasks. A little repetition is okay. Otherwise, a better strategy is to say "good dog" or some other positive thing when your dog is hesitant.

The hard dog, on the other hand, quickly takes such flexibility as meaning they don't have to react until the second or third repetition. It is hard to know when to stop repeating commands and to start demanding immediate action. Generally speaking, by the third repetition of a lesson, your dog should not need to hear a command more than once, provided it is given clearly and with the correct cues. From time to time I break this rule if I see a dog becoming unduly stressed and showing fear when the material is presented to them. Since this is more common among juveniles than mature dogs, I often cut more slack with the young ones. Being too demanding too quickly can burn out a young dog. However, being too slack makes for a sloppy performance. The point is, you don't have to turn the screws all the way in the early going. You have the option of repeating a lesson another day for the express purpose of improving a performance.

The majority of dogs have little trouble with these commands, until they get to the distraction phase of the training. The more work you can do with distraction, the better your dog will be during the off–leash phase. Vary the location of your training sites and vary the types of distraction presented to him. The hardest test is usually the presence of another dog. There you are, getting along famously, when some stray brute comes upon you and your training partner.

Don't panic when this happens. Keep your attention focused on your dog. Speak to him and use your voice to encourage him or to warn him when it looks like he might break. Ignore the other dog and correct yours if he steps out of line.

When I was 13 I had a partbred Basenji. He was perhaps one of the greatest personalities I have ever owned and a boy's best friend. A Basenji isn't a very big dog and neither was Nikki; but in spite of his size he really liked to scrap. Normally, Nik was super obedient, except when it came to other dogs, particularly males. We disagreed about that more than all the other bad things he did, combined . . . well, that's not entirely true. He used to disappear for about two weeks every spring and, after a few years, there were an awful lot of dogs that looked like him in the neighborhood. We never actually disagreed over this little idiosyncrasy but I worried about it and certainly should have stopped him . . . I just didn't have any idea how, since he could open the front door as well as I could.

*"Nikki"*

Shortly after I got Nikki from the city pound (where I am sure he had been arrested for going walkabout), I took him for a walk in the nearby park on a leash. We hadn't been there long when a good-sized German Shepherd (about twice the size of Nik) came trotting up to us. I didn't know what to do, so I hung on tightly to the leash. Within a matter of seconds, they went at it. I kept trying to pull Nik away but every time I did, the shepherd would close in for the kill and soon had Nik by the throat. There was a tremendous amount of confusion, noise and blood. I finally regained my wits and made a grab for the shepherd, whereupon, I got bit too. In spite of the injuries, my involvement convinced the shepherd to run away.

From then on, I never grabbed my dog when the fighting started. I always went after the newcomer. At least I could control Nikki and usually the other dog left us alone when it looked like he might have to fight two. Later, I got a bit smarter and would make threatening gestures and noises at the intruder and Nikki alike, which usually averted any further contests.

I can't stop without telling one more story about the time Nikki was almost cured of fighting.

I would take Nikki for walks in the park, off leash. He was pretty good about coming to me when I called and would only take on a dog if he came too close to me. One day, we encountered another dog. When I called Nikki to me, the other dog followed, taking Nikki's retreat to be an invitation for more aggression. When Nikki got to within 10 feet of me, he suddenly reversed himself and set upon the other dog. Not much happened because both the other dog and I were so surprised by such a sudden turn of events. The other dog ran off without any resistance.

On the way home, Nik was acting as cocky as could be. He was always cocky but this was extreme. I was still miffed at losing control of him so suddenly but still not smart enough to put a leash on him. He spied a pair of Siamese cats on the porch of a house we were passing by. In an instant, he was on the porch after those two cats. I don't know what he thought he was going to do, but I do know things did not work out as he planned.

One cat retreated to the back of the porch and turned to face him. The second cat jumped on Nikki's back from the railing. The first proceeded to close ranks with the second. By the time I got to the porch, both cats were having a fine old time and Nikki was trapped on the porch by the railing. I didn't try to bale him out this time. I was too busy trying to get out of there myself.

Nik took quite a beating that day and for the next couple of months, he was good as gold about not fighting or running away. I never did break Nik of his desire to play the tough guy and right up until he died 11 years later, he still was always looking to mix it up.

How much distraction you expose your dog to should be governed by the successes and failures of previous experience. If you have had some success with mild distraction, try the harder stuff. If you had trouble the last time out, go back to the basics before trying it again. Use your long line always, because a breakaway at this stage will teach your dog a strategy for avoidance you would rather they didn't know. The long line allows you to afford your dog the luxury of making choices without having to risk losing control. I should have figured that out while I still had Nikki.

# Chapter Three Test
# Lie Down, Stay and Come

Yup. It's that time again. Remember, the idea here is not to humiliate you in front of family and friends. The idea is to confirm whether or not you and your buddy are ready to go on to the off–leash work.

This is also a time for you to recognize how much progress you and your partner have made since starting this little project. Recognize too, how much more you are enjoying your dog and how much of a personality he is. The fact is, you understand your dog much better than you did before and because of this, you can identify his emotions and enjoy his company far more than can a person with a disobedient dog.

Here is your assignment (should you choose to accept)

1. Develop a routine that incorporates all the skills practised from Lesson 5 to 7 inclusive. This routine will be about 8 – 10 minutes long. It should include Lie down, Sit, Come, Lie down–Stay, Sit–Stay and Heel. at the minimum.

2. Pick a location with moderate distractions, such as a park near a high-traffic area. The location should contain children, traffic noise, new sights and smells and possibly other dogs, provided they are on leash.

3. Have a friend watch your routine. They should mark down each time you are required to give a voice or leash correction. Have them indicate what command was failed.

For example:

| Command | Number of Corrections | Voice/Leash |
|---|---|---|
| Heel | 0 | NA |
| Sit | 1 | 1V |
| Down | 3 | 2V/1L |
| Sit–Stay | 1 | 1V |
| Down–Stay | 1 | 1L |
| Short–Stay | 0 | NA |
| Long–Stay | | |

If you were required to give fewer than five corrections during your routine, you pass with flying colors. As in the Chapter Two test, if you had to give more than five corrections, you should try to analyze where the problems are. Spend a few more days working on these problems and then move on to the next chapter. As you work through the next chapter, be conscious of what areas of your program might be weak and spend a bit more time on the long line.

# 4

# Off Leash

The lessons covered in this chapter are a bit different from the previous ones. We will not learn anything new in the sense of introducing new skills. Instead, we will try to extend control over our dog in terms of distance and time. The difficulties we encountered will not be so much teaching a particular manoeuvre but teaching that obedience is expected *without* the aid of a leash or physical connection. The connection will be a mental one.

This chapter is designed to cover the skills acquired in previous lessons. The only difference is that, this time, you will not have a leash to control your dog. The Heel, Sit, Come, Lie down and Stay are all covered. Therefore, it might be a good idea to review earlier lessons that pertain to these skills before you start off–leash lessons.

A friend of mine once said, "Did you ever wonder why convicts continue to make escapes from jails when the guards have all the advantages?"

I said, "No, but I'll bite – how come?"

He said, "Because the convicts have nothing else to do but think about it, while the guards have very little time to think about it."

With that titbit of useless information, I would like to pontificate on the subject of off–leash training. Think of them as Rules to Win By, if you like.

## NEVER HESITATE TO CHEAT

While this rule might get you shot in a card game, it works well when it comes to training dogs (provided they don't know about card games). I think my friend might be right about convicts. I am almost sure he is right if you apply that same principle to dogs. They do think about what you did with them yesterday and they are not above outsmarting you if you don't pay attention.

What I am really talking about here is the need to continue to plan. Think about how to gain an advantage and how to set up your training situations so that you don't get outsmarted. If you see an opportunity to take advantage, use it.

## NEVER HESITATE TO RETREAT

Sound military advice to be sure. If things aren't going your way, go back to the leash work for a while. Repeat an exercise that didn't work off leash. This time use the leash or long line. While this isn't as satisfactory as not having trouble in the first place, it is a good compromise strategy.

## NEVER GIVE UP

There is a neat poster going around at work these days with that title on it. It shows a picture of a big bird with a frog in its mouth. The bird can't swallow the frog because the frog is choking the bird. Sounds kind of silly when you think about it. The point is, you may not have things turn out exactly the way you planned. In fact, you may have an outright "wreck" (to use a technical term). As long as you keep trying, planning and pursuing the level of performance you desire, you will win. After all, how smart can this damned dog be anyway?

Let's get down to the "How To" of the matter. Remember, the principles of off-leash training are the same as before. Pressure and relief, correction and praise, anticipation and cues are still fundamental to the program. This time, however, you have to rely on voice more than physical contact to provide these things. Some other tools in your bag of tricks are eye contact, habit or the familiarity of a routine and the firm notion that you are the pack leader. You have been relying on these tools for some time now. Soon, you will be even more dependent on them.

# Lesson 8
# Off-Leash Heel

This is going to be a piece of cake. You can do this in your sleep – but don't. Be aware of the fact that your dog can get away from you so gradually you might not notice. The next thing you know, he is heeling (sort of) several feet away and is starting to cast about for something else to do. The key here is, be picky. Start with the straight line work and demand that your dog maintain the same position he does when he is on the leash. Correct him when he strays. Many trainers use a short line on the choke collar. It is a piece of line about 6 – 8 inches (15 – 20 cm) long. It allows the trainer to reach to the collar and give a leash correction if required. If your dog is not particularly responsive to voice corrections, go ahead and put a short line on.

## I. Lesson Plan

There are two objectives this lesson should meet. The first is the obvious one; to have your dog heel correctly (at least as well as on leash) through the basic heel routine. The second purpose of this exercise is to begin to establish off-leash control while doing an exercise your dog is very familiar with (heeling).

In this series of exercises you do not want any distraction in the early stages. Try to find a location that can contain your dog, in case he should happen to break away. At the least, pick a location well away from traffic.

Start with some straight line work, much in the same fashion as when introducing the heel on leash. Keep the pace fairly even and easy to follow. Above all, demand that your dog maintain position.

After a one to two minutes of the easy stuff, start to vary your speed and make the exercise a bit more challenging by changing direction. Don't make it too difficult but make it interesting or your dog will quickly become bored and start to lose his concentration.

When your dog falls out of position, immediately apply correction. Generally speaking, if a dog is falling behind, I encourage him to keep up by saying "good dog" and so forth. If he starts to get ahead or off to the side, I growl "Nooo." If I think the cause of falling behind is an attempt to avoid the exercise, I verbally correct with a warning growl followed immediately with a correction using the short line on the collar. If I continue to struggle with position, I put the leash on and proceed for a minute using the leash to provide correction. Once I am satisfied with his on-leash performance, I go back to off leash for one to two minutes of harder work.

## Correction Before the Fact

As you move through the off-leash exercises, try to improve your ability to anticipate when your dog is going to need correction and apply a little pressure at that time, instead of after the fact. Pressure will normally take the form of voice warning. Body language and eye contact are also useful. **The ability to anticipate allows you an opportunity to provide your dog with the chance to avoid correction altogether**. This subtle technique is likely one you have noticed already. The fact that you no longer have the leash to rely on makes it that much more important in controlling your dog. *Anticipation* is the key to maintaining contact with your dog, because the application of correction after you have lost contact is not nearly as effective as catching the transgression before it happens.

As an example of anticipation, consider how your leash worked during the heel sessions. If Quincy wasn't terminally stupid, he figured out exactly how long your leash was early in the game. He discovered that heading West while you were going East hurt his neck, but only after he had already gone West for a little while. In time, he developed an understanding of just how much slack was in the leash and therefore, was able to anticipate when his neck was going to get hurt. This anticipation permitted him to make a decision about whether or not to maintain position **before** he received correction. Without the leash, you have to take an even greater role in determining how much slack to provide with respect to position. My recommendation is, not much. Warn your dog verbally at the first instant of deviation. His anticipation of additional correction will convince him to correct himself before going any further.

Another part of this lesson plan is the issue of **distraction**. Some people like to leave the distraction work to near the end. The rationale for this is that they have firmly set all the commands necessary before running the risk of having a dog break away.

I have tried this method and it is adequate. But I prefer to introduce distraction much earlier. I use it to test my control at the end of most lessons. I have two reasons for doing this. The first is that it takes several weeks to thoroughly ground a dog in the obedience skills and during that time a lot of distractions come up that I don't have any control over. If the dog already has been exposed to some distraction, these unexpected incidences will not unduly upset my training.

The other reason for starting distraction early is because leaving it to the end of a dog's training cycle comes as too big of a shock. There isn't a chance to increase the amount and variety of distraction gradually.

Either way it's not a big deal. You can choose to leave the distraction work to the end of this chapter or you can introduce it at the end of each lesson in this chapter. I have included some discussion about distraction in the remaining lessons, in case you decide to introduce distractions this way.

### II. Execute the Plan

The first repetition of Lesson 8 – Off-Leash Heel, should be done with as few distractions as possible. Pick a location where you can easily catch your dog if he should get away.

Perhaps a fenced backyard would be good. Any further repetitions should be in locations where a bit more risk is involved.

Step 1. Do about half a minute of heel work on leash. Be sure to correct quickly and authoritatively if required. Take the leash off and continue in a straight line for up to 75 yards (70 m). Begin a few slow turns; first inside, then outside turns for about two minutes. Stop from time to time and ask your dog to sit. Heel away, remembering to start off with the correct foot. During this period, keep a fairly even and easy-to-follow walking pace.

Step 2. Practise changing your pace, all the way up to a jog. Start off with straight-line work and introduce the turns after you are sure that your dog is able to maintain his position.

Step 3. Make your turns more abrupt. Go from jog to stop several times. Have your dog sit during each break. As in the on-leash portion of this type of work, the fast pace is mentally hard on your dog. Rest frequently and keep it short. About one minute of this work followed by another half minute of rest usually feels about right. A total of three to four minutes of actual work is a long time and time to quit.

Step 4. This part is optional, as discussed earlier. I like to expose my dogs to distraction in small doses. Here is an opportunity to choose a location with distraction and repeat Steps 1 and 2. If you would like to try Step 3 with distraction, do it after a day's rest.

## Summary

The trick to this lesson is to maintain contact with your dog. Don't let him slip away while you are watching where you are going. Easier said than done! Obviously, you have to take your eyes off him from time to time or you'll break your neck. You can span these moments by talking to him. A running chatter of "good dog," "keep up" and "atta boy" will serve to keep you in touch. Of course, Quincy will soon learn that you are not watching, if this is the only time you talk to him, so try to be vocal during the whole of the exercise.

The most common mistake made during this phase of training is getting too confident. Usually, your dog will perform very well. You become so pleased with the results that you start to take him everywhere off leash. Then one day you encounter a distraction you hadn't planned on. If it is too powerful a temptation and you lose your dog, you have taken two giant steps backward. If you are really unlucky or if you make this mistake repeatedly, your dog will develop the breakaway as an avoidance strategy. He'll be too smart to fool with the leash and will know exactly when he doesn't have it on.

### Off-Leash Breakaways

If you happen to run into trouble with a dog that breaks away while off leash and yet is too smart to give you trouble while on leash, try letting him drag the long line while you do your off-leash work. Don't rely on the long line too much. Use it only when he makes a concerted attempt to break away. For corrections, stay with your voice and use the short line for leash correction. The long line simply makes a clean getaway more difficult. If/when he makes a break for it, don't call him until just before he runs out of line. I am assuming in this case, that you've already used your warning voice and he has ignored it. Step over and pick up the line, give him one more warning "Nooo" and then bust him! This is a very bad deal and a habit that must be broken immediately. It is extremely unlikely that fear is the cause of this strategy – but it should be considered if you have been pushing him too hard. Most likely this is something he has discovered by accident and has decided to try again. Stop it as soon as you can.

The final word on dogs that break away is walking them down. We have discussed this in Lesson 6. It is unpleasant, frequently dangerous (car traffic, etc.) and to be avoided if at all possible. Try to stay within the limits of your command while in the presence of distraction. The place to extend the distance over which you have control is on the quiet confines of a training ground. New distractions should be added while on leash.

# Lesson 8
# Off-Leash Heel

### Juvenile and Mature Dogs

Copy this sheet and take it with you. Check off the items as they are completed.

_____ lesson plan completed

_____ locations selected (with and without distraction) – locations are safe?

_____ reviewed previous skills (i.e.) on-leash heel

_____ Heel exercises completed properly (with and without distraction)

_____ you were able to anticipate incorrect behavior

_____ voice correction/warnings given properly

_____ overall training time should be about 10 minutes per session

_____ repeat this lesson at least twice (for a total of three)

# Lesson 9
## Stay

———

The more you repeat the Heel sessions from Lesson 8, the better. The reason for this is that part of the point of the exercise was to establish off-leash control and the Heel exercise is the easiest way to do this. The more you repeat the sessions, the more control you will have for these other exercises. If you run into difficulties in this lesson, try repeating the Heel – Lesson 8, a few times before coming back to this one.

Review some of the things we discussed in Lesson 6 – Stay (on leash). The procedure is going to be pretty much the same. Presumably, you used the long line for Step 4 of Lesson 6. Therefore, this seems like a good place to start this lesson.

While we may start with the long line, which will give us about 40 - 60 feet (12 – 18 m) of control, we would like to finish this lesson with a dog that will stay from distances of over 100 yards (90 m) and for periods of at least three minutes. The addition of both distance and time makes this lesson much more challenging than the previous Heel lesson. It means that you repeat your stay command many times during each session. Each time, you are trying to add a little more distance or a little more time before you recall your dog.

How far you take this exercise is, of course, up to you. I think that three minutes and 100 yards is reasonable for most people, most of the time. However, there is no particular limit to how long or from how far away you can practise this command. If you wish to develop this command further than what we will do here, then by all means do so. It is simply a matter of more repetitions.

A word of caution if you decide to make this a marathon event. During the course of extending the Stay, you will find that the risk of a breakaway is directly proportional to both distance and time. Therefore, you will put greater pressure on your dog. You will increase the risk of getting hung up on this skill to the exclusion of others. You will find yourself fighting for control. All of this is fine – provided you have a reason for doing it. But, if you have no practical application for this skill, you will have taken this risk for no good reason . . . why do it?

## I. Lesson Plan

Building on what we have already accomplished in Lesson 6, we will start with the long line work. From the Heel position, command your dog to "Lie down." Give the Stay command. Remember to put your hand to the dog's nose and lead off with the right foot. Walk away a short distance, stop and return to your dog. By mixing this exercise with a bit of heel work and adding distance and time over many repetitions, we will eventually get to where we can have a dog stay from a reasonable distance and for a reasonable length of time.

This lesson is one of the longer ones – often up to 20 minutes in length. The reason for this is that, as we practise the Stay, we are expending time. Normally, 10 minutes of a lesson is 6 – 8 minutes of hard work. The Stay command is not hard work. Therefore, your dog should be able to handle the longer lesson with little or no difficulty.

You should try to vary time, distance and the position (Lie down vs. Sit) you set your dog in. Whether you start with Sit–Stay or Down–Stay should be of little consequence at this stage. Sooner or later you are going to want to be able to do both. The important things to remember are that (1) you do not want your dog to anticipate your next command and (2) you want to have him waiting for your recall for as long as it takes.

I will provide you with a set of steps that add distance and time to your Stay command. However, this will be only an outline. You will want to add variations of your own as you go through the exercises. You may find that I am going too fast in progressing through the steps. That is okay. Simply put some filler exercises in between the steps to help with the transition. Treat your dog as the individual he is. Modify the training exercises to suit both of you.

## II. Execute the Plan

Step 1. Complete an off-leash Heel routine for about two minutes to take some of the air out of your dog. Once you feel he is settled, attach the long line to his collar. Throw the line off to the side. It is only for emergencies. If your dog is already in the Sit position, command "Stay." Walk away about 10 – 20 feet. Stop and face him. Wait another 15 – 20 seconds and then walk back to him. During this time, watch him carefully. If at any time he looks as though he might break, give him a warning with your voice. If necessary, put your hand out like a traffic cop or point at him, as well as using your voice. Try NOT to repeat your Stay command. Once you have returned to your dog's side, heel away for perhaps 40 – 60 feet (12 – 18 m). Stop and repeat the exercise. Add another 10 feet (3 m) and 10 seconds to your stay.

Step 2. Repeat this exercise four times. Use Lie down–Stay and Sit–Stay twice each. Each repetition should add 10 feet and 10 seconds on to the waiting time.

Leave your dog in position with a Stay command. Walk straight away for about 20 feet (6 m). As you continue past 20 feet, start to walk left or right (your choice) until you are standing off to your dog's side (either 9 o'clock or 3 o'clock position). Retrace your path back to your dog. As you repeat this exercise, alternate between Sit and Down and walking left or right. Your dog should continue to face straight away and not turn to face you as you move around him. Should he do so, correct him with your voice. Don't make a big deal of this if he insists on turning as you do. He will stop doing it once he gets used to it. Do continue to try to correct his positioning.

Step 3. Repeat Step 2 several times. Continue to add time and distance as desired. This time, walk all the way behind your dog (6 o'clock position) on at least two occasions. Have him get thoroughly used to you moving around and away/toward him as he continues to Stay. Vary things as much as you can. For instance, make your circles wider as you walk around him, then oblong, then straight away, then away and towards him and so on. Walk 30 – 40 yards (27 – 37 m) away and sit down yourself. Remove the long line from his collar at some point during this exercise. Be prepared to put it back on if you start having trouble. Otherwise leave it off.

Step 4. Repeat Step 3 at least two more times. This time, try to get out of your dog's sight. Go around the corner of a building or whatever. Stay out of sight for at least one minute before returning to your dog's side. Finish these exercises with some easy Heel work.

Step 5. Change the location of your training site to something with a bit more distraction. Put the long line back on for the first part of this exercise. Repeat Steps 1 – 4 at least once each. Notice which distractions your dog finds the most tempting and expose him to more of it when you know you can catch him if he breaks.

You may wish to expose your dog to a variety of locations and distractions. The more the better, as long as you continue to control the situation.

## Summary

As was the case with Stay (on leash), the juvenile dogs often struggle with Stay off leash a bit more than mature dogs. Recognize that this is mostly a case of youthful exuberance and not anything particularly bad. The youngsters frequently have a difficult time sitting still for any extended length of time. Are your kids any different? (Mine weren't.)

You will find that juvenile dogs often require more repetitions of these exercises before they can be considered "steady." For these situations, I keep the long line attached for a few extra repetitions – just to be safe.

You have the option of doing a great deal of ground work on this command or relatively little, depending on how important it is to your situation. I strongly believe that out of sight or 100 yards (91 m) distance for three minutes duration is plenty for the average dog.

The breakaway is, of course, your biggest concern in this lesson. I have had a number of dogs who were fine as long as they could see me but would break when they could not. Be innovative! There is nothing stopping you from getting a longer line or enlisting the help of a friend. Each dog and each situation is a little different so it is difficult for me to predict exactly what you should do when faced with a breakaway situation. This is where you have to get devious and outsmart your opponent. One thing is for sure – you cannot let it become a habit or an avoidance strategy.

# Lesson 9
# Off-Leash Stay

### Juvenile and Mature Dogs

Copy this sheet and take it with you. Check off the items as they are completed.

_____ lesson plan completed

_____ locations selected (with and without distraction) – Locations are safe?

_____ reviewed previous skills (i.e.) on-leash heel

_____ Stay exercises completed properly (with and without distraction)

_____ you were able to anticipate incorrect behavior

_____ voice correction/warnings given properly

_____ overall training time should be about 20 minutes per session

# Lesson 10

# Come

---

This lesson should be incorporated into future repetitions of Lesson 8 and 9. In Lesson 9, each time you concluded a Stay session, you returned to your dog's side. In this lesson, you alternate between returning to your dog and recalling him (command "Come here.") As you progress, add a number of variations such as: Stay–Come here, Lie down–Come here, Sit–Come here. Such a combination of commands, given in rapid succession, will fine tune all of them.

As a final fine-tuning exercise, I think you should try putting at least two of these commands on to whistles (more about this later). It is easy to do and will add a great deal of distance to your sphere of control. Whistles can usually be heard at distances of a mile or so. Many (if not most) dogs will take a whistle command with greater consistency and speed than voice commands. There are a great variety of whistles to choose from. I use a small plastic device called a Shepherd's whistle. It gives much the same sound as whistling through your teeth. Other types of whistles are also useful. The ones that give a high-pitched sound are better than the ones that do not because dogs seem to hear them better. Whistling through your teeth is great because you can use a variety of tones and pitches. One of the great failings of my youth was that I could never whistle through my teeth. I'd put my fingers in my mouth and blow for all I was worth but no sound ever came out . . . I was so disappointed!

## I. Lesson Plan

Training your dog to come under controlled circumstances is the best way to develop a steady dog – one that can be recalled at any time. On the other hand, controlled circumstances behavior does not necessarily mean that your dog will come under uncontrolled situations. One way we can develop that skill is by practising in the presence of distraction. Another way is to recall your dog for no particular reason other than to practise. The lesson plan will not address this last method since it is designed to be a rather spontaneous thing. The spontaneous recall is a good exercise and should be done whenever/wherever it occurs to you. Watch you do not set yourself up for failure by spontaneously recalling your dog at a time when you know he is not likely to obey. Like the Stay command, Come here needs to be developed through a series of gradually more challenging situations.

In the following exercises, the idea is to place your dog in position and move away from him while he is told to "Stay." Over a series of ever-increasing distances, you will call your dog to you, instead of walking back to him every time.

Once sufficient distance is made between you and your dog, you may practise stopping him with commands such as "Lie down" or "Sit" before recalling him the rest of the way to your side. It is also at this time that I usually introduce whistles for both Come here and Lie down.

The Lie down whistle is almost universally a long, high-pitched blast that tails off at the end. The Lie down whistle is usually held for two to four seconds, thus giving the dog time to stop and lie down before the command is finished. When practising the Down whistle, make sure that the ground will not hurt your dog or make him reluctant to take the command. Gravel and pavement should be avoided. When introducing the down whistle, give the whistle, take one step toward your dog and give the "stop" hand signal (traffic cop, hand straight out), all at the same time. Follow this immediately with the voice command. Do this several times, after which you can delay the voice command and instead repeat the whistle and follow with a "Nooo" if he doesn't take the command . . . then repeat the voice command and take another step toward him. (All this has to happen within a few seconds in order for it to be effective, so practise it a few times without the dog in order to get it straight.) After about 6 – 10 repetitions of this, your dog should at least stop when he hears the whistle. It may take several more repetitions before he starts to go down immediately upon hearing the whistle.

The Lie down whistle is extremely useful. I have been able to save the lives of several dogs because they would obey it from great distances. I can recall three or four instances when my dog would have been run over by a vehicle if I had not been able to stop them with a whistle. It is also very useful for getting out of a wreck. There have been several occasions where the dog has managed to escape my control (particularly when herding cattle) and I was able to stop him with the whistle before he ran the cattle through a fence.

The Recall, or Come here whistle, is equally useful. Although there is much greater variation in whistles for a Recall command, most use a modulated, sustained whistle. For example, the whistle a construction worker might use to attract the attention of a woman is often called a "wolf whistle." I know several trainers who use the wolf whistle, repeated at least twice, as a Recall signal. It meets the criteria of a good recall signal in that it is high pitched, modulated and distinctly different from the Lie down whistle. You can invent your own Recall whistle. The key thing to remember is that it should be distinctly different from the Lie down whistle.

The Recall whistle is easier to teach than the Lie down whistle because all you have to do is go to the end of your long line, blow the whistle command and tug on the line. After a few repetitions, delay tugging on the line for three to four seconds, to give your dog time to obey. The procedure is exactly the same as what you did the first time you taught Come here. The only difference is that now you are using the whistle instead of the voice command.

Any time you are required to work your dog from a distance, whistles give you a significant advantage. The use of whistles is common among many of the trainers of working breeds, particularly the shepherds and the gun dog trainers. You are by no means limited to the above two whistle commands. If you felt like it, you could put your whole repertoire on whistles but the two mentioned are particularly useful.

## II. Execute the Plan

Step 1. Take your dog to your quiet training location. Practise your Heel exercise for a couple of minutes. Practice the Stay routine to review what you did the last time out. Do this several times until you are comfortable, the dog is steady and you have at least 30 yards (27 m) of distance between you and your dog. After each session, return to your dog.

Do it again. This time, when you tell your dog Sit-Stay or whatever, only go about 20 feet (6 m) away, wait 10 – 20 seconds. Give the command "Come here." If your dog has a history of being reluctant, you might want to do this with the long line the first few times. When he comes to you, have him "Finish" so that he is back in the Heel position. "Heel away" for a few yards. Stop and repeat the exercise.

After you have done this exercise twice, start to alternate between recalling ("Come here") and returning to your dog. That way, he will not be able to anticipate the recall and therefore be less likely to break from the Stay command.

If your dog starts to hesitate about coming on the recall, give him a lot of encouragement when he does start toward you and for the next three or four times, use the recall instead of walking back to him.

If your dog starts to anticipate the recall, do not recall him for the next three or four times. Instead, walk back to him. Also, do not always "heel away". Sometimes, it is useful to walk back to your dog, say nothing and then walk away again. The trick is to put enough variation into your routine so that your dog does not begin to anticipate your next command and jump the gun, and yet not so much that you totally confuse him!

If you want to use the whistle for recall, now would be the time to introduce it. This will mean you will have to add several more repetitions to the routine. You may want to spread this step out over two or three days but it shouldn't take you much longer than that. You can also practise the Recall whistle in your home between sessions, spontaneously.

Step 2. Add distance to your routine. Starting from 20 feet (6 m) away, add 10 – 20 feet (3 – 6 m) each repetition until you can recall him from about 100 yards (91 m) away. Remember to keep mixing it up. (Otherwise he will start to break on you.) Rely on your whistle as much as possible so that he gets familiar with it.

Step 3. Starting from about 30 feet (9 m) away, recall your dog from the Stay position. When he is about 15 feet (4½ m) away, give him the Lie down command. Remember to take a step toward him and put out your hand at the same time. You want him to take this command immediately, so be PICKY! After the first few times, I drop the hand signal and body language stuff.

This is also the time to introduce the Down whistle. Practise it at close range. You may have to add the body language/hand signals back into the program for awhile.

If you are having any trouble with him, put him on the long line loop. As discussed in Lesson 7 – Come, by running the long line from his collar, around a post and back to his collar, you have your dog under control in a manner that allows you to correct either the Come command or the Lie down command. Practise "Come here" followed by "Lie down" when he is about 10 – 15 feet (3 – 4½ m) away from you, until you have it perfect. If you are going to go to all the trouble of setting up the loop, you might as well use strictly whistles for this exercise.

Step 4. Add distance and variety to the routine. As you get further away from your dog, practise putting him "Down" (or "Sit") at various points along his recall line. Oh, I forgot . . . when you command "Come here," your dog is supposed to come to you on an imaginary straight line – I call it the "recall line." Deviations from the recall line should be corrected. When you command your dog to Lie down or

Sit, he should maintain his position on this straight line. When you get enough distance between you and your dog, you might try a string of commands such as Come here–Sit (wait 10 seconds)/Come here–Lie down (wait 20 seconds)/ Come here–Finish . . . Heel away. Each time you command "Come here," give your dog time to get up and come at least 20 feet (6 m) toward you before issuing the next command.

Keep your string of commands from getting too predictable. From time to time end a string with Sit (or Lie down) and then walk to your dog. Three or four of these strings in a 10 minute training session is plenty. Watch for signs of confusion or mental exhaustion. Once this exercise stops being fun for your dog, he will tire quickly.

Practise walking around your dog in a big circle. When you get to a position, say 3 o'clock, try recalling him from that point a few times. Practise recalling him from a variety of positions as you work your way around your Sit-Stay dog. You do not need to do this often but it is a good idea for your dog to learn to recall from positions other than straight away from you.

Also, in your attempts to add variety into your routine, don't forget to practise Stay for differing lengths of time. Incorporate time into your routine as another variable.

Step 5. Pick a location that offers distraction. Without getting too carried away (you old show off you!), practise parts of your routine where your dog has the opportunity to be distracted. Be careful! What may have been a flawless performance without distraction can turn into a wreck in a hurry. Start with the simple stuff and work your way up to the more challenging. You can progress fairly quickly since this is all review by now. I like to tempt my dog a few times before I am prepared to try the long-distance work. Wait until he has had some distraction at fairly close range before you leave him at the local Fair in the Sit-Stay position.

As unlikely as it may be, perhaps you are finding it difficult to locate areas for training that are both reasonably safe and afford some measure of distraction. Do not hesitate to set up distracting scenarios to tempt your dog. Friends, neighbors and even total strangers can occasionally be coerced into role playing to give you the chance to test ol' Cool Hand Luke. If you don't normally encounter distraction, create a situation. If you are going to go to all the trouble of setting your buddy up, make it a good one. Manage the situation so that you get the maximum benefit from both the transgression and the correction. Be creative and offer the finest in temptations.

## Summary

This is one of my favorite stages in the training cycle. It marks the beginning of the end of Basic Training. Completion of this final lesson will provide you with a friend you can be proud of. More importantly, you have given your dog the discipline he needs to remain mentally healthy for the rest of his life – not to mention the fact that obedient dogs tend to live longer. From here on, you will need to be more innovative to find challenges for your teammate.

On the other hand, you do not want to "short circuit" him by applying more pressure than he can handle. You need to be shrewd in your assessment of your dog's capabilities in order to avoid going too far, too fast. Should you succeed in getting ahead of your dog, he will begin to make mistakes. He may try avoidance tactics such as breaking away. He may begin to show signs of mental stress that lead to confusion and an apparent inability to deal with simple commands. I have seen some especially good juveniles look brilliant in the early going, only to crash and burn in these latter stages because trainers put too much pressure on them. While the juvenile is the most likely to suffer from this problem, mature dogs are by no means immune to it. Don't be so busy having fun that you forget your buddy. He is relying on you for his mental health.

One of the best things a trainer can do is to build his or her dog's confidence. We have talked a great deal about how YOU can win in what is basically an adversarial situation. Somewhere around Lesson 6, you began to grow beyond the WE versus THEY attitude. You and your dog have become a team. In keeping with that idea, you need to concentrate more on what your dog is doing right and less on what he might be doing wrong.

A well-respected horse trainer once remarked to me that it was his intention to set up every situation so that it was easy for his horse to do the right thing and difficult for him to do the wrong thing. I believe that the same can be done with dog training. When your dog gets used to doing the right thing he gains confidence. He gains pride and he is having fun. He becomes less willing to do the wrong thing and more willing to try new things. Set your training sessions up with the idea that you both can win. The reward is a dog that cannot "short circuit" and will not stop trying to please you.

# The Final Test
# Putting It all Together

---

We in the peanut gallery salute you! Putting it all together means displaying all the skills you and your partner have mastered – a bit of a show, if you will. Invite your aunts and uncles, friends, spouse and children to witness a miracle . . . okay, a nifty graduating exercise.

Develop a short (five to eight minute) routine to demonstrate the range of skills you and your dog have acquired. Put about two minutes of your best leash work together. Use your imagination. Be a little artistic if you like. Show your Heel work – high speed, crisp turns and military-like precision. Conclude this section with a Sit–Stay (while you catch your breath).

Proceed to the off-leash work. Demonstrate Heel, Come, Finish, Sit, Lie down and Stay. Invent some distractions to amuse and amaze your audience. Perhaps the finale might be a recall from a long distance followed immediately with a string of commands given on the whistle.

Fireworks are optional.

# Postscript

I hope you have enjoyed this little project as much as I have enjoyed writing about it.

The conclusion of this book need not be the end of your training fun. Indeed, the end of basic training is the beginning of a host of other challenges for you and your partner. Most of the countries I have been in have a Kennel Club. These clubs have carried obedience training and competition far beyond what we have covered here. The easiest way for you to locate a Kennel Club in your area is to contact your local veterinarian or write to one of the organizations on page 141. These folks will likely be able to put you in touch with the right people.

As man's best friend and most popular pet, the number of organizations that promote, judge, discuss, enjoy and even fawn over dogs are almost endless. I encourage you to participate in any one or several of these – you have a lot to offer. I am of the opinion that dog people are good people. I like to socialize with them. So will your dog.

There are many breed-specific clubs. Likely a club specializing in your area of interest exists not too far from you. Gun dogs, guard dogs, lap dogs and yes, sheep dogs, abound in great numbers. Subscribe to one of the dog magazines and attend a breed show. Pet stores are often a good source of information. Your local library will be able to show you other avenues to follow.

You may have discovered a life-long hobby. I can only hope you enjoy it as much as I do.

There is a certain kinship among trainers – welcome to the fold! If you find an overwhelming need to contact me, I can be found at:

suttont@vm.lakelandc.ab.ca

on the E-mail trail.

Good Luck to you both.

# Glossary

Note: While all the terms to follow have a proper definition, I thought it might be handy to provide you with an explanation of what these terms mean in the context of this book and in particular reference to dog training.

ANTICIPATION. To realize beforehand that a particular action is about to take place.

AVOIDANCE TRAINING. A process whereby a dog learns to avoid pressure by performing an action before the pressure is applied.

BODY LANGUAGE. Non-verbal communication through means such as expression, body-stance and movement.

COMMAND. To issue an instruction or set of instructions to your dog.

CONFINEMENT. To restrict your dog's living environment to a particular place or area. Usually, this implies a space approximately 100 square feet (or 10 square metres).

CORRECTION. To suppress inappropriate behavior by providing the dog with an unpleasant experience and (where possible) encouraging appropriate behavior with a pleasant experience almost immediately thereafter. A correction is most effective when both positive and negative reinforcements are used. A good correction not only points out what is wrong but also how to do the action correctly.

CUE. A hint on which your dog is to act. An indication to your dog that it is his turn to do a certain thing. A cue usually precedes a command.

DISTRACTION. An object or action that serves to divert your dog's attention away from its intended focus.

ELECTRIC COLLAR. A dog collar that contains a receiver and a transmitter that is held by the trainer. When operated by the trainer the collar is capable of emitting either a sound or electrical shock, or both. The more sophisticated of these are capable of both positive and negative reinforcement.

HARD AND SOFT DOGS. The inherent sensitivity of a specific dog to pressure. This is often reflected in the amount of stress a dog experiences during training and determines how much pressure a specific dog can withstand during a training session. This term is an attempt to separate environmental influences on behavior from genetic behavior determinants. A hard dog is generally considered more resistant to pressure while a soft dog is not.

HEEL. This command instructs the dog to maintain his position at your heel while waliking, jogging or even standing still. You should be able to move without tripping over your dog and not lose contact with him.

"HEEL AWAY". Slang term referring to the act of commanding your dog to heel while at the same time walking away.

IGNORANCE. Uninstructed or uninformed. The dog is unaware of what is being asked of it and therefore does not know how to complete the task.

LONG LINE. A long length of cord (40 – 60 feet or 15 – 20 metres) that may be attached to the dog's collar or leash and acts as an extension to a leash. It is used to provide control over a greater distance than a normal leash.

PRESSURE. The continued application of force. In training terms, the use of pressure usually involves relatively mild force for the purpose of causing stress. The intended reaction to this stress is for the dog to seek and find relief or release by completing a desired command. (Sometimes called "AVOIDANCE TRAINING").

PUNISHMENT. To inpose a penalty for a fault or crime. This book attempts to differentiate between punishment and correction in that punishment relies solely on negative reiforcement for the purpose of changing a behavior. *See also* CORRECTION.

RECALL. To bring back. Verbal commands such as *Come* or *That'll Do* are synonymous to a recall.

"RECALL LINE". Imaginary straight line that your dog is supposed to follow when coming towards you.

REINFORCEMENT. To strengthen by adding material. In this context we intend to strengthen a behavior through additional stimuli. Negative reinforcement refers to unpleasant stimuli intended to decrease incidences of inappropriate behavior. Positive reinforcement refers to pleasant stimuli intended to increase incidences of appropriate behavior.

SHEPHERD'S WHISTLE. A small piece of plastic or metal that when fitted into the mouth and air is forced through emits a high pitched whistle, similar to whistling through your teeth. It is used to convey commands over a long distance.

SOCIALIZATION. The process of learning how to live and effectively function in an organized community in a cooperative manner. The implication is that your dog will learn how to function in the community of humans and other dogs in which it lives

SOFT DOGS. *See* HARD DOGS.

The American and Canadian Kennel Clubs are national organizations that are great sources of information. If you are looking for specific information related to dog issues or would like to find out about a Breed Club in your area, the AKC and CKC are good places to start. Feel free to contact them as they may provide access to one of their affiliates nearby.

American Kennel Club

5580 Centerview Drive

Raleigh, North Carolina 27606

USA

(919) 233-9767


Canadian Kennel Club

100 - 89 Skyway Avenue

Etobicoke, Ontario

M9W 6R4

Canada

(416) 675-5511 /Fax (416) 675-6506